Going Bush

Adventures Across Indigenous Australia

lonely planet

MELBOURNE · OAKLAND · LONDON

Contents

Tropical

Mountains & Plains

Introduction

Imagine just doing this every day for the rest of your life. I could definitely do that —just stay here and send a post card every now and then to the folks back home: 'Cath and Deb have gone bush'. —Deb

Whether you're looking for adventure, ancient rock art, an insight into a profound indigenous culture, or just a bloody good yarn, nowhere else in the world holds a richer bag of discovery than Australia. With this book as your inspiration, choose a getaway car and plot a rough course off the beaten track to a high-octane adventure across the red heart and true soul of Australia.

Australia's vast and varied landscapes are epic. In these pages you'll find ancient outdoor art galleries, cattle stations the size of small European countries, sunbaked landscapes with bloated boab trees and seemingly endless kilometres of staggeringly beautiful coast. Roads as long and straight as the horizon lead to cool oases and shady valleys. Weird and wonderful rock formations resembling something from outer space nestle in boundless national parks thousands of kilometres wide or just beyond the edges of the city.

This is a country where nagging flies pester visitors out of complacency. Where the culture has its own distinctive quirks, ranging from a beanie festival in Alice Springs to world lizard-racing championships in Cunnamulla. Where you can share a cold beer with nuggety characters or sample some witchety-grub salad. It's a country with a history full of contrasts: diving for pearls in Broome and mining for iron ore in Mount Isa, heartbreaking stories of early exploration such as the ill-fated Burke and Wills expedition, and the deep-rooted spirituality of the Aboriginal Dreaming woven into the very landscape. Australia has many stories, scars and scenic wonders. Discover the folk hero Jandamarra, an Aboriginal police tracker turned freedom fighter; Wolfe Creek Crater, the second-largest meteorite crater in the world; and the Quinkans, knobbly characters depicted in the rock-art galleries near Laura. But don't make the mistake of thinking it's just about the outback: this is a big country, and though there are 7,682,300 square kilometres of Australia to explore you don't have to go far to find its essence. Stunning natural beauty and fascinating indigenous heritage are at your feet, even in the middle of a golf course in the country's biggest city. And accessing this unique fusion of adventure and cultural spirit is as easy as veering off the well-worn tourist path.

Australia's indigenous peoples are part of the very fabric of the country. They have the longest continuous cultural history in the world, with origins dating back to the last ice age. Australia originally contained at least 600 different societies, each with its own dialect, culture and traditions. While most Australians now live in the coastal regions of Australia, historically Aboriginal peoples lived in all areas of the country, many of them in the desert. They also lived along the coast or on the island of Tasmania, among the inland mountains and plains, or in the northern tropics, where Torres Strait Islanders shared cultural influences with the Aborigines of the mainland. This book has been structured according to these broad geographical regions, which, despite some overlap between the regions and many small differences within them, largely influenced the lifestyles, food, accommodation and beliefs of the peoples living in them.

This book began when Catherine Freeman and Deborah Mailman took a road trip across northwestern Australia from Broome to the tip of Arnhem Land for Lonely Planet Television. We were inspired to create a book that showcased the incredible places they visited. But we didn't stop there: we went on to cover every skerrick of the Australian bush, from Coober Pedy to Cape York and Tasmania to Tennant Creek.

City slickers Cath and Deb found themselves exploring terrain that was as unfamiliar to them as it is to the average traveller. Going bush gave them a chance to explore and celebrate their own country as well as getting closer to their indigenous heritage. Along the way, they hooked up with local indigenous travel guides and tour operators who gave insights into the landscape, bush foods and local language, or took them to the rodeo and showed them how wild the bush can be.

As they discovered, on the road the only constraint is a seatbelt. You're otherwise free to design each day, choosing from Australia's remarkable range of elements. Away from the time-pressured constraints of the city there's no need for nine-to-five – the bush prefers to sync up with the weather, with chance and opportunity. An Australian road trip is the epitome of the old clichés: it really is as much about the journey as the destination, and travelling far from home often leads you closer to yourself.

So follow Cath and Deb's example and get out there – whether you're dragging a caravan, steering a high-clearance four-wheel drive or riding in the back of a bus. With an elbow out the window and the crooning lilts of Jimmy Little (honoured on Tamworth's country music Roll of Renown) floating out of the stereo speakers, you'll hope the passing kilometres never end.

Catherine Freeman

Catherine is one of Australia's most admired and respected athletes, best known for winning an Olympic gold medal at the Sydney Olympic Games. Now retired from professional track and field, she remains an international personality and role model.

I was born in Mackay, central Queensland, and I've been residing in Melbourne since 1991. The great thing about being retired from professional track and field is that I don't have to travel abroad as much; I get to enjoy being Australian and understanding what that means to me.

I've had a very nontraditional indigenous upbringing. My grandmother, my mother's mother, was forbidden from speaking our native Kuku-yalanji language. So, along with the language went the whole culture of my nanna and of our siblings. It's unfortunate because there's always a sadness at losing your sense of belonging to a culture. Because of my stepfather's job as a jackaroo we moved around loads – all over Queensland. I went to ten different schools, including two boarding schools. But I'm very much a city girl these days. I don't speak any other language. I've definitely spent most of my time in the mainstream of Australia, so there was a huge part of me that was really looking forward to learning more about my indigenous culture.

I think to be Australian you need to appreciate the bush and I've always been proud of my indigenous heritage. But I've been too busy doing other things in my life to really get a good understanding and grasp of traditional indigenous culture in modern society today. So, this trip was a lot of fun for Deb and me, learning together. I learnt a lot more about the ways in which my ancestors used to live. In my role as a public person, people look at me and they see an indigenous Australian woman, so I want to be able to speak confidently about the traditional ways.

Deborah Mailman

Deborah is one of Australia's most popular and successful actors and is often recognised for her portrayal of the much-loved role of 'Kelly' in the television series The Secret Life of Us. She has a swathe of stage and screen credits to her name.

I am an urban black, a city girl, even though I don't want to be but I've been in the city for so long now. But coming back to the bush is reminiscent of having grown up in Mount Isa. I instantly feel relaxed, I feel calm, and that's what I was really looking forward to in the time that we spent out bush: no stress and just enjoying meeting the people.

From this trip I definitely got a deeper understanding of my mob – my people, and indigenous culture, a better under-standing of the stories that come from this part of the coun-try. It was a bit of a cultural awakening for me to be honest, and a very spiritual trip as well. And the other great bits were meeting people, eating a bit of fish and having some good tucker!

It was great travelling with Cath. It's been good medicine for her, without the pressures of public life and the city. She handled those roads like a professional: she can drive that girl! It's been great being in the car; she's hitting those pot-holes at eighty kilometres an hour and loving it. You can see that she just wants to be a part of it – she's not afraid to get in and try new things. That's what it's all about.

Coastal

The breathtaking silhouette of Mount Coonowrin at dawn Photo: Richard I'Anson

The Family of Mountain Spirits: Southeast Queensland Coast

Queensland's surf 'n' sun strip is one of the country's favourite holiday spots. But it's not all about martinis and bikinis – local indigenous communities are preserving their rich cultural inheritance and also looking to the future. The region is home to some unique Aboriginal farming ventures that you're welcome to visit.

About twenty kilometres north of Caboolture, the Glass House Mountains are a curious group of volcanic crags sticking up from the coastal plain. Aborigines believed these peaks to be a family of mountain spirits.

According to legend, Tibrogargan noticed that the sea was rising one day, and gathered his children to flee to safety. He ordered his son Coonowrin to help Beerwah, his mother, who was heavily pregnant, but Coonowrin fled, shaming his family. Tibrogargan punished him with a club

on the head, which broke Coonowrin's neck, giving Mount Coonowrin its distinctive crooked outline. Tibrogargan stares eternally out to sea and away from Coonowrin, unable to contemplate his son's lack of courage. The many streams running off the mountain are the family's tears of shame.

There are a few sites of interest in the area, including axe-grinding grooves two kilometres south of Landsborough, a well-preserved bora ring (a circular ground used for ceremonies) at Glass House and a midden at Mission Point.

In the Sunshine Coast hinterland, Cherbourg Aboriginal community was set up by the Queensland government as a forced Aboriginal settlement in 1904 and is now owned by a community trust.

WHERE
Queensland's Sunshine
Coast stretches from the
top of Bribie Island to
Noosa.

WHEN
Try to visit in summer for
the very popular Woodford
Folk Festival (07-5496
1066), held annually
from 27 December to 1
January. It is a major focus
for indigenous performers,
musicians, storytellers, artists and craftspeople from
around the country.

HOW
Ferryman (07-3408 7124)
on Bribie Island runs cruises through Pumicestone
Passage Marine Park and
can show you an extensive
midden at Mission Point.
The commentary relates
the wildlife and ecology of
this outstanding area to the
traditional inhabitants.

Making a splash at Sunshine Beach Photo: Oliver Strewe

Off the rack: laid-back attire at Eumundi Market in the Sunshine Coast hinterland Photo: Richard l'Anson

Take a stroll around to see the town's murals and then head
over to the main attraction – Cherbourg Emu Farm. Queensland's first commercial emu farm supplies breeding stock
to other emu farms and emu meat to restaurants. The farm
is open to the public and has displays of hand-carved emu
eggs and fine emu leather.

Further north at Hervey Bay, Korrawinga Aboriginal community runs Scrub Hill community Farm. This former cattle
ranch is now a self-sufficient community producing organic
vegetables, tea-tree oil and Aboriginal art. You can take a
tour of the community, which includes a bush tucker and
medicine trail.

Fancy footwork at Woodford Folk Festival
Photo: Simon Foale

Goanna à gogo: mural in Nimbin Photo: Mark Andrew Kirby

Ceremonial Lands: North Coast NSW

A gorgeous coastline, excellent nightlife and a laid-back attitude has made a pilgrimage to Byron Bay almost obligatory for young Australians. And this area has been host to important rites of passage for millennia. There are many important ceremonial places in the region, including the mysterious Nimbin Rocks. This is also a good place to see bora rings – circular areas ringed in banked earth to create a sacred space for rituals.

There's a bora ground in Tweed Heads, behind the Minjungbal Aboriginal Cultural Centre, which was a traditional ceremonial site and dance circle for men. The centre also has shields marked with spear dents on display and turtle shells that were used as baby cradles.

Sixteen kilometres south of Lismore is another bora ring, which has now been incorporated into the Tucki General Cemetery on a hill overlooking the Richmond River valley. Initiation ceremonies were held here and it is a very significant site – be careful not to disturb anything when you visit.

About twenty-five kilometres north of Lismore, the Nimbin Rocks are three thick stalagmite-shaped peaks, clearly visible from the road. The rocks are a very sacred men's site connected to a clever spirit man called Nyimbunji (probably the source of the name Nimbin). *Our Land, Our Spirit: Aboriginal Sites of North Coast New South Wales*, published by the North Coast Institute for Aboriginal Community Education, says that 'initiated men wanting to take tests to become "clever" men could go to the site to train in the occult, ventriloquism, psychology, magic and hypnotism. They could become invisible, turn into their totems, heal illnesses, ward off evil spirits or magic death spells'.

All painted up: every body has a story **Photo:** Becca Posterino

Beach bums soak up the sun in northern New South Wales **Photo:** Peter Ptschelinzew

WHERE
This area occupies the far northeast corner of New South Wales.

WHEN
Music lovers should try to make it here in Easter for the East Coast Blues and Roots Festival (www .bluesfest.com.au), which traditionally has a strong indigenous component. Note that prices in this region skyrocket in summer and at Easter.

HOW
Ngulingah Local Aboriginal Land Council (02-6621 5541) in Lismore can organise bush tours and storytelling if you ring in advance. There's an art and craft shop on the first floor selling woven baskets, T-shirts and ceramics.

The land around the rocks belongs to two local Aboriginal communities, and is off-limits without their permission to enter.

Further south, between the Pacific Highway and the coast, Bundjalung National Park is almost 4000 hectares of coastal land, with thirty kilometres of unspoilt beaches for surfing and swimming. Named after the traditional owners, the park's extensive middens and old camp sites indicate it was a popular spot. You can take the Gumma Garra walk to see a scar tree (a tree from which bark has been removed to make canoes, shields and other items).

While in the area, drop by Gurrigai Aboriginal Arts & Crafts, which has a huge range of items for sale, including books, cosmetics and crosshatch paintings from Arnhem Land.

Let there be light: the moon over Cape Byron Lighthouse **Photo:** Holger Leue

The Dreaming:
Spiritual Links to the Land

The beginnings of Aboriginal Australia have their roots in the Dreaming, when ancestral spirit beings travelled across the country, creating humanity and the natural environment, customs and laws, songs and stories. As the Dreaming ancestors travelled, they sang into creation the rocks, mountains, trees and rivers; they took the form of humans and animals and travelled everywhere, entering the earth and sculpting the landscape, creating natural features we still see today. The great fish swished its huge tail and splashed the water, making the bends in the river as it travelled to where the river meets the sea. The ancestor spirits cried and made the natural springs from their tears, and the great snake travelled all over the land, forming the great life-giving underground and inland rivers. These Dreaming stories crisscross every part of this country in a web of 'songlines'.

Just as there are hundreds of different Aboriginal languages spoken across Australia, there are also hundreds of different Aboriginal cultures and spiritual beliefs. However, all Aboriginal people have a common belief in the Creation, or the Dreaming. They believe they are descended from the Creator beings of the Dreaming and that their ancestral relations teach them about the unity they share with all things in the natural world. In Aboriginal spirituality all animals and plants are equal, and humankind is just one part of the overall cycle of life. For indigenous Australians, the Dreaming is a continuing time, not a time in the past. The Dreaming is in the past, the present and the future.

Just as they care for members of family, indigenous Australians are also obliged to care for their ancestors who dwell in the land. The land is sacred because it carries the footsteps

of the spirit ancestors as they walked every part of it, laying tracks and spiritual songs. The land is sacred because the essence of Aboriginal spirituality lies in the earth: spirit guides are resting in the mountains, in the rocks, in the rivers. The significant Dreaming places in the land are known as sacred sites. The creative powers of the ancestors are thought to be alive and to influence all things still in the natural world, and if these spirits are disturbed, so too is the cycle of life and the natural order. When sacred sites are destroyed, Aboriginal Australians believe their ancestors are disturbed and will no longer protect or provide for the people. A damaged or destroyed sacred site may result in natural disaster, and sickness may afflict communities who have not fulfilled their cultural obligations as custodians. Indigenous Australians believe that by neglecting their spiritual and cultural obligations they bring disharmony to the country and the community.

For Aboriginal Australians, the idea of the land being *terra nullius*, or a vast empty space across which people range sporadically, is a myth. They know the land intimately: every rock and every river has a name and is remembered in the Dreaming, as it is still remembered today. To own the land as a piece of real estate, as a 'property', is an idea remote to indigenous people. Their relationship to the land is much more complex. The idea of Aboriginal ownership is not exclusive but rests in a group of people, and does not define the owned object as a commodity that can be traded or sold. The role of indigenous Australians is at once that of traditional owner and custodian of the land, and carries with it both rights and responsibilities. The land and everything in it must be protected and sustained; for example, there may be a particular obligation not to kill the females of a certain animal species, in order

to preserve the species. When traditional custodians or owners approach their country they communicate with the spirit ancestor of the place. They tell the ancestors who they are and introduce anyone whom they may have brought with them to the place. When food is taken from the land, thanks is given to the ancestors. Nothing is assumed or taken for granted – not even the next meal. Aboriginal Australians always seek permission from the spirit world for their actions.

The boundaries between different Aboriginal clans or nations are sometimes marked. These boundaries are not straight lines but may be determined by the footsteps and tracks of the ancestors and marked by bends in the creek or river, the rain shadow, trees and rocks. Some regions were shared between different Aboriginal peoples and some

were restricted, but permission was always sought to travel across the country.

Some of the rights and responsibilities of custodians are made known to the members of an Aboriginal community through songs and ceremonies. Aboriginal laws and spiritual beliefs are not written down; their knowledge is passed on from one generation to the next through their dances, songs, stories, dreams and paintings. The songs are a record of their culture, their history, their laws, and lay a path to follow. Song is the universal order; the singing of songs ensures the continuity of life, abundance and harmony.

Ceremonies are an integration of song, dance, art and mime, a time when the best dancers and singers become

the ancestral beings and re-enact the activities of the ancestors. Ceremonies honour and celebrate the ancestors and the Dreaming, offering an opportunity to maintain and protect the spirit places of the ancestors. They regenerate Aboriginal communities, acting as reminders of their roots and expected behaviours as set down in law by the ancestors. They provide a forum for the settling of disputes that may arise over land, marriages, hunting and gathering rights, and a whole range of community conflicts. They are also a celebration for the renewal of life, and the changing of the seasons.

Aboriginal law and spirituality is a layered system of knowledge. Some knowledge can be made public, while other layers of information and knowledge are secret and sacred. Those initiated in ceremonies or who have had the know-

ledge passed on directly to them keep sacred knowledge. Some of the men's ceremonial business is never revealed to women, and some ceremonial business of the women's law is never revealed to men or to the public at large. Secrecy provides a means of protecting and maintaining knowledge of the law and spirituality in a respectful way that is in accordance with Aboriginal protocols.

In Aboriginal eyes, law, culture, spirituality and the land are seen as one entity. Spirituality comes from the Dreaming ancestors, whose spirits are alive in the land. Their spirituality was sung to them in the Dreaming and is still sung across the country today, by the ancestors with the rising of the sun. Law, culture and spirituality is sung and is alive in all things. Aboriginal spirituality, land, life and laws are all interconnected: all is one and one is all.

Rockin' it at the Vee Wall graffiti space, Nambucca Heads **Photo:** John Borthwick

A Landscape of Creation Stories:
Coffs Harbour Region

From the adventure sports of Coffs Harbour to the hippy haven of Bellingen, this stretch of the New South Wales coast is steeped in Aboriginal legends. You can retrace the steps of the Creator spirits who shaped the land during the Dreaming.

The best way to visit the many Aboriginal sites north of Grafton is to take the Lower Clarence Aboriginal Tourist Site Drive, a self-drive trip that takes in thirteen significant Aboriginal sites. The drive begins at the Maclean Lookout, with the story of the giant serpent that travelled up the Clarence River, shaking off barnacles that became the different tribes in the area. It ends at the Woombah Midden, reputed to be the largest midden on Australia's east coast (a 3000-year-old dingo tooth was found here).

In the nearby Gibraltar Range National Park there is a walking trail to the Needles. According to one legend, these six granite outcrops are six sisters who were turned to stone by their pursuer's curse.

Further south, at the Yarrawarra Aboriginal Corporation in Corindi, you can see how fish were traditionally caught in a rock pool when there were two tides in one night, and two nearby middens, which are around 1000 and 4000 years old respectively. You can also visit an 'ochre-trading place' and even paint yourself with ochre markings.

Nambucca means 'crooked knee', and the town of Nambucca Heads is named after a young warrior whose knees were bent when he was speared to death, at what is now prosaically the site of a caravan park.

West of here is the small township of Bowraville, home to a large Aboriginal community.

Home to roost: Muttonbird Island, Coffs Harbour **Photo:** Richard l'Anson

WHERE
This region is on New South Wales' mid-north coast.

WHEN
High season is summer and school holidays, particularly Christmas, January and Easter. You can save money on accommodation by avoiding these times. Catch the Coffs Harbour International Buskers' Festival (www.coffshar bourbuskers.com) in late September. Watch tattooed men balance precariously on a unicycle, while juggling bearded ladies with chainsaws in one hand and nonchalantly eating an apple and directing traffic with the other hand.

HOW
Contact the Coffs Harbour Visitors Centre (02-6652 1522) for detailed information on tours in the area.

The award-winning, ecofriendly Mountain Trails (02-6658 3333) runs four-wheel-drive rainforest, waterfall and bush-tucker tours in the Coffs Harbour region.

All tied up at Coffs Harbour Marina **Photo:** Richard l'Anson

If you take a real shine to the Aboriginal stories in the area, visit the Durahrwa centre in South Grafton. This nonprofit community organisation showcases the work of local artists. It also produces ceramics decorated with local stories.

Bananas grow all around Coffs Harbour **Photo:** John Banagan

21

Bare Island Fort at La Perouse, Botany Bay, was built in the late 19th century to fend off potential invaders from Russia **Photo: Ross Barnett**

The Art in Urban Rock: Sydney Region

Australia's biggest, brashest city has a secret treasure. Hidden away on secluded rock faces is the world's greatest collection of urban rock art. The engravings are 'pecked' rock carvings, which were made by painstakingly striking the rock with a sharp stone, then joining the pecked marks into a groove. The finest sites are just outside Sydney at the Ku-ring-gai Chase, Brisbane Waters and Royal National Parks.

The outcrops of relatively soft Hawkesbury sandstone in Ku-ring-gai Chase National Park are smooth, even and relatively easy to engrave. The Basin Track, at West Head in the park, is probably the best interpreted rock-engraving site close to Sydney. It features images of fish, a row of hopping wallabies and life-size human figures in outline with just eyes for details. The first engraving you come to is a group of four figures; the largest man has raised arms

and is holding a boomerang and a fish. In the last engraving site is a figure with arms outstretched and wearing a belt and necklet.

Nearby, the circular three-and-a-half-kilometre Garigal Aboriginal Heritage Walk takes you to a shallow rock shelter adorned with red-ochre hand stencils. The next site features an engraving of a man with no neck and no internal details.

Brisbane Waters National Park, north of Ku-ring-gai Chase, contains the Bulgandry Aboriginal Engraving Site. The most unusual feature of this site is a man depicted wearing an elaborate headdress, carrying a sword and club or small boomerang, and seemingly about to step into a canoe. Another engraving is a kangaroo with what looks like either an octopus or spider over its tail.

No textbook can give you the same detail as actually seeing it there. -Deb

Jogging the memory at an Aboriginal rock art site in Bondi Photo: Michael Laanela

Melting the ice at the Bondi Icebergs Pool Photo: Dallas Stribley

South of Sydney, the site at Jibbon Point, in Royal National Park, includes rock engravings of kangaroos, whales and a six-fingered male figure who could be one of the mythical spirits that feature in coastal Aboriginal stories.

There are also some sites right in the city, including engravings of a large whale and a man holding a fish at Bondi Golf Course, another whale on the clifftop walk between Bondi and Tamarama and more carvings on the eight-kilometre Manly Scenic Walkway between the Cutler Road Lookout and Grotto Point.

Fish and a boomerang almost collide in this Aboriginal rock engraving at North Bondi Photo: Paul Beinssen

WHERE
The rock art of the Sydney region in New South Wales extends from Royal National Park in the south to Brisbane Waters National Park in the north.

WHEN
The wettest period in Sydney is March to June, so this is the worst time for bushwalking. It's well worth timing your visit to go to the Survival Day concert at Waverley Oval, Bondi, on 26 January.

HOW
A Field Guide to Aboriginal Rock Engravings by Peter Stanbury and John Clegg is widely regarded as the most authoritative layperson's guide to Aboriginal rock-engraving sites in and around Sydney. The Metropolitan Local Aboriginal Land Council's *Footprints on Rock: Aboriginal Art of the Sydney Region* by T and N Popp and Bill Walker looks at the historical and cultural context of various sites.

Darkingjung Local Aboriginal Land Council (02-4351 2930), in Wyong, can arrange guides for the sites in Brisbane Waters National Park and parts of Yengo National Park, which forms part of the Greater Blue Mountains World Heritage area and is of cultural significance to local Aboriginal groups.

The Bundeena–Maianbar Heritage Walk in Royal National Park offers good coastal views and some Aboriginal sites of interest. For a tour with an Aboriginal guide, call the visitors centre on 02-9542 0666.

23

Looking for love? Female satin bower birds are attracted to the male with the fanciest bower **Photo:** David Curl

Coastal Colours: South Coast NSW

Arthur Boyd, the celebrated Australian artist, chose New South Wales' rugged south coast to set up his studio near Nowra – today his former home at Bundanon is an arts centre where you can take workshops. This wild coastline has inspired many other artists, and it's a great place to visit Aboriginal art galleries and see artists' work. It's also possible to sneak a peak at areas usually closed to the public by taking a tour with a local Aboriginal guide.

Start your art tour in Wollongong, where you can see the work of Jerringha artist Lorraine Brown in the *Gurungaty Fountain*, built in 1997 to commemorate thirty years of Aboriginal citizenship. Brown also created the mural at Beverley Whitfield Pool in nearby Shellharbour.

While you're in town, drop by the Wollongong City Gallery, which has a good collection of paintings, including bark

paintings from Arnhem Land and dot paintings from the Western Desert.

In Huskisson you can visit Laddie Timberys Aboriginal Arts & Crafts, which displays and sells work produced on site by the local Koori community; there's also a boardwalk through wetlands here.

Small Wallaga Lake National Park, near Bermagui, takes in most of the western shore of a beautiful tidal lake at the mouth of several creeks, and has prolific bird life as well as protected middens. There is no road access, but you can join an excellent tour of the area with the local Yuin people through the Umbarra Cultural Centre. Boat cruises take in sacred sites such as Merriman Island, and there are also tours to Mount Dromedary and Mumbulla Mountain, both of which are of great spiritual significance to the Yuin.

WHERE
New South Wales' south
coast extends from around
Wollongong to the Victorian
border.

WHEN
This stretch of coast is
popular during Christmas,
Easter and school holidays,
especially the month of
January; accommodation
will cost less at other
times.

HOW
Bundanon (02-4422
2100) is in Cambewarra
West, southwest of Nowra.

In Akolele, Umbarra
Cultural Centre & Tours
(02-4473 7232) has a
retail outlet and a museum
display.

Barry's Bush Tucker Tours
(02-4442 1168, 0410
744 744), in Booderee,
offers short tours.

Angling from the wooden bridge at Wallaga Lake Photo: Ross Barnett

The centre has arts and crafts for sale, and you can join in
hands-on activities such as ochre painting and boomerang
throwing.

Wreck Bay is a closed Aboriginal community in Booderee
National Park, which occupies Jervis Bay's southeastern
spit. Much of the park, which is jointly administered by the
Wreck Bay Aboriginal community and Environment Australia, is heath land, with some forest, including small pockets
of rainforest. Although you can't visit Wreck Bay itself, you
can experience some Aboriginal culture with a local guide
on Barry's Bush Tucker Tours. Barry will teach you about
the seasons and local plants, and loves a yarn around the
campfire. Afterwards you can explore the bush by spotlight,
witnessing the habits of nocturnal creatures.

Youngsters playing in the surf at Tuross
Head on the south coast of New South
Wales Photo: Ross Barnett

Golden sunrise over the Gippsland Lakes **Photo:** Greg Elms

On the Lizard's Trail:
East Gippsland

Gippsland has some of the most diverse wilderness, scenery and wildlife on the continent, bristling with national parks, lakes and deserted coastline.

This is the land of the Kurnai, descendants of their Dreaming ancestors, Borun the Pelican and his wife Tuk, the Musk Duck. The best way to take in the major sites is by joining the Bataluk Cultural Trail, which follows a network of Kurnai trails and trading routes. The route takes its name from the Kurnai word for lizard, and is a self-drive trail. The trail begins at Ramahyuck District Aboriginal Corporation, which has a small display of locally made crafts, including screen prints, some of which are for sale.

The next stop is at Knob Reserve, Stratford, where axes were sharpened by the Avon River (Dooyeedang). Then it's over to the spooky Den of Nargun in Mitchell River National Park. According to Aboriginal stories, this small cave is haunted by a strange, half-stone, half-woman creature – the Nargun. According to legend, the creature would drag passers-by into her cave and, if attacked, was able to deflect spears and boomerangs back onto the thrower. It's believed that the legend developed from the whistling sound of the wind in the cave, and served the dual purpose of keeping Kurnai children close to camp sites and scaring others away from this sacred place where women's initiation ceremonies were held. A one-hour loop walk leads to a lookout, rainforest gully and the den. It's not possible to enter the cave.

The trail then takes you to Howitt Park, in Bairnsdale, where there's an interesting scar tree. The scar is four metres long and about 170 years old. From here the trail

Cascading water at Amphitheatre Falls, Toorongo Falls Reserve Photo: Paul Sinclair

This ancient rock formation in Royal Cave, Buchan, is at least 300 million years old Photo: Patrick Horton

goes to Metung, on the shore of Bancroft Bay, to visit the sacred site of Legend Rock. According to Aboriginal stories, the rock represents a hunter who was turned to stone for not sharing the food he had caught. There were originally three rocks, but the other two were destroyed during road-construction work, and the remaining one was saved only with the help of community pressure. Metung is also an upmarket base for all sorts of water-based activities, including sailing, cruising and fishing.

The trail goes on to visit Buchan Caves; Burnt Bridge Reserve (near Australia's first successful land-rights claim at Lake Tyers); a Kurnai plant-use trail through Orbost Rainforest; and a shell midden at Cape Conran.

Great lakes: Gippsland's lakes are ideal for boating Photo: Sara-Jane Cleland

Rounded granite boulders tinged with orange lichen at Oberon Bay **Photo:** Paul Sinclair

Breathtaking Bushwalks: Wilsons Promontory

One of the most-loved national parks in Victoria, the 'Prom', as it's known by locals, was established in 1898 and covers the peninsula that forms the southernmost part of the mainland. The Prom offers a superb variety of activities, including more than eighty kilometres of walking tracks and a wonderful selection of beaches – whether you want surfing, safe swimming or a secluded spot, you can find it at the Prom. Then there's the wildlife, which abounds despite the park's popularity.

The plentiful wildlife was one of the drawcards for Aboriginal people of the Kurnai and Boonerwrung clans, who called the Prom Yiruk or Wamoom respectively. Aboriginal associations with the area date back at least 6500 years, and there are middens and artefact scatters at many places, including Cotters and Darby Beaches, and Oberon Bay. The Dreaming stories of Lo-errn, Bullum-Boukan, and the Port

Albert Frog all mention that the area and the park once formed part of the land bridge that allowed people to walk to Tasmania.

You don't have to go very far from the car parks to get right away from it all. The walking tracks take you through swamps, forests, marshes, valleys of tree ferns and long beaches lined with sand dunes.

The top five walks are the Great Prom Walk, a moderate forty-five-kilometre circuit taking two to three days; the Lilly Pilly Gully Nature Walk, an easy two-hour walk through heath land and eucalypt forests; the Mount Oberon Summit walk, a moderate-to-hard walk of two and a half hours with panoramic views; the Little Oberon Bay walk, an easy three-hour walk over sand dunes; and the Squeaky Beach Nature Walk, a five-kilometre stroll through tea trees and banksias

Home away from home **Photo**: Bethune Carmichael

View towards pristine Picnic Beach **Photo**: Christopher Groenhout

WHERE
Wilsons Promontory is 200 kilometres southeast of Melbourne (Victoria) via the South Gippsland Highway. The main visitor facilities are at Tidal River, thirty kilometres inside the park.

WHEN
Summer (December to February) is the high season, when the park is at its busiest and local accommodation is more expensive. On the plus side, from November to Easter a free shuttle bus operates between the Tidal River visitors' car park and the Mount Oberon car park – a nice way to start the Great Prom Walk.

HOW
The Wilsons Promontory National Park office (03-5680 9555, 1800 350 552) is in Tidal River.

Numerous outfits run tours in the park – check the Parks Victoria website for details.

to a white-sand beach (go barefoot on the beach to find out where the name comes from).

The beach at Norman Bay is safe for swimming and is a fantastic spot for families. You've also got a great chance of spotting some wildlife. There are over thirty species of land mammals in the park, including wombats, the long-nose potoroo, the feather-tailed glider and the eastern pygmy possum.

The nearest settlement to the Prom is Yanakie, an Aboriginal word meaning 'between waters'. It's easy to spot eastern grey kangaroos, wombats and emus in the grasslands nearby.

A crimson rosella fossicks in the grass
Photo: Regis Martin

The You Yangs rise out of a grassy plain **Photo:** Chris Mellor

Buckley's Chance: Geelong Region

A runaway convict who talked in tongues, a pride of lions in an Australian bush setting and the rock walls of Wurdi and Ude Youang await you in this incredibly diverse region.

This is the region where runaway convict William Buckley famously moved in with the local Wathaurong tribe in 1803 and stayed for thirty-two years. You can follow his adventures on the William Buckley Discovery Trail that runs from the granite peaks of the You Yangs Regional Park to Aireys Inlet, southwest of Geelong at the start of the Great Ocean Road's coastal run. It takes in six important sites detailing the story of the 'wild white man', including Point Lonsdale, where he is thought to have sheltered in a cave under the cliffs.

Buckley was absorbed into Wathaurong life, so much so that he had forgotten how to speak English by the time he encountered John Batman's party in 1835. At Yollinko Park Aboriginal Garden, on the Barwon River in Geelong, you can see the tools that he may have learned to use in the form of some impressive larger-than-life sculptures. This is a great place to picnic, and there's also a shell midden and traditional indigenous garden here.

In the You Yangs, reliable water supplies are scarce. Aboriginal people enlarged natural hollows in the rock so that they would retain water even in the dry months. You can see these rock wells at Big Rock in the You Yangs. The strange name of the granite peaks comes from the Aboriginal words Wurdi Youang and Ude Youang and means 'big mountain in the middle of a plain'.

Further south, on the Melbourne (eastern) side of Anglesea, the one-kilometre Point Addis Koorie Cultural Walk features

Deserted shoreline near Bells Beach **Photo:** John Banagan

A mob of kangaroos gathers on the ninth at the Anglesea Golf Club **Photo:** Bernard Napthine

interpretive signs with information on local Aboriginal people, plants and animals. Take some water and stick to the tracks, as the terrain can get slippery. There's a rewarding ocean view from the lookout where the walk concludes.

South of Geelong is the Werribee Open Range Zoo. This vast free-range park set in bush land features lions, zebras, hippos and other African animals.

You can learn more about the local Aboriginal community by dropping into Narana Creations in Geelong, where there's a gallery, shop and native garden, or Wathaurong Glass, which offers a range of fine glass products, including kiln-formed and sandblasted pieces.

A wooden lifeguard lends a hand at Cunningham Pier, Geelong
Photo: Chris Mellor

WHERE
Geelong is a one-hour drive southwest of Melbourne, Victoria.

WHEN
Summer (December to February) is the most popular time to visit. The last week of January is Skandia Geelong Week, Australia's largest sailing regatta, when over 400 yachts compete in an event that began in 1844.

HOW
Werribee's Open Range Zoo (03-9731 9600) is west of Melbourne on the way to Geelong.

The Geelong & Great Ocean Road Visitors Centre (03-5275 5797) has information on the William Buckley Discovery Trail.

The indigenous-owned and -operated Wathaurong Glass (03-5272 2881) is in North Geelong.

Two of the Twelve Apostles watch over the Shipwreck Coast **Photo:** Richard I'Anson

Gunditjmara Warriors: Shipwreck Coast

Over 700 vessels lie crumpled on the ocean floor of south-west Victoria, including the *Loch Ard*, which was wrecked near the region's most famous attraction – the Twelve Apostles – hence the name 'the Shipwreck Coast'.

This terrifying coast passes through the land of the Gunditj-mara people, who saw it in a very different way. With their intimate knowledge of the land and sea, the Gunditjmara thrived on the coast that was so treacherous to newcomers, and fought fiercely against the incursions onto their lands.

Near Warrnambool, towards the western end of the Great Ocean Road, you can visit the Tower Hill Natural History Centre. Set on an extinct volcano, this centre has a small pictorial display describing local Aboriginal history. Also on display is a collection of indigenous artefacts, including a

stone-grinding dish and hand axe. Some of the Aboriginal relics found by archaeologists in this area precede an eruption of the volcano at Tower Hill some 30,000 years ago.

On the outskirts of Warrnambool and overlooking the sea, Thunder Point Coastal Reserve has middens (accessible by a walking track) believed to be between 3000 and 7000 years old.

Griffiths Island (or Maleen, as it is known by the Gunditj-mara) is accessible by a short causeway from Port Fairy. The island has self-guided walks with interpretive signs about local Koorie history. The main walking track is named after Tarteel, the last Aboriginal chief of Maleen. The island also has Australia's largest mainland shearwater (mutton bird) colony.

Because y'are surrounded by all of this natural beauty, you immediately feel calm. – Cath

Footprints on the beach near the Twelve Apostles **Photo:** Bernard Napthine

WHERE
The shipwreck coast stretches from Prince-town, close to the Twelve Apostles, to Port Fairy in southwestern Victoria.

WHEN
Whale-spotting is possible from around June to September, particularly between Warrnambool and Port Fairy. Mutton-bird season on Griffiths Island is from mid-September to late April.

The Tarerer Festival, held in the Warrnambool area each January, showcases indigenous and nonindigenous local musicians. The concert is officially opened by local Elders and has a focus on Reconciliation.

HOW
The Tower Hill Natural History Centre (03-5565 9202) is fifteen kilometres northwest of Warrnambool.

Eumeralla Backpackers (03-5568 4204) is in Yambuk.

The Framlingham Aboriginal Trust (03-5567 1003) is about twenty kilometres northeast of Warrnambool.

Lady Julia Percy Island (Deen Maar) is about eight kilometres offshore from Port Fairy. This sacred island is the resting place of the spirits of the dead from the Gunditjmara people. The flat-topped volcanic island is also where Bunjil, the Creator spirit of southeastern Australia (the creator of humankind according to the Wurrunjeri people), departed this world.

Beyond Port Fairy is the blink-and-it's-gone town of Yambuk. Middens found in the limestone cliffs east of Yambuk reveal that Aborigines lived here over 2000 years ago. There's a good lake for fishing and the spacious Eumeralla Backpackers, run by the local Framlingham Aboriginal Trust. It has good facilities and canoes can be hired to paddle down the Eumeralla River to the lake. Ask here about tours to a deeply spiritual place at Yambuk that has walking trails and a lake. The lake attracts many birds, including the rare orange-bellied parrot. The property, which is undergoing a revegetation programme, has access to a beautiful stretch of secluded beach where you can watch the wild waves.

Coastal vegetation and Island Arch at Loch Ard Gorge **Photo:** Grant Dixon

The remains of an old jetty project out into the clear waters of Lillies Bay, Wybalenna Photo: Richard Eastwood/APL

Wybalenna – Black Man's House: Flinders Island

Visitors to Flinders Island, in the wild Bass Strait, are almost spoiled for choice. The island has beautiful beaches, good fishing and abundant wildlife. Scuba divers have the chance to explore the many shipwrecks offshore and bushwalkers can scale the peaks of Mount Strzelecki.

But there's also a poignant side to visiting the island, due to its tragic history. Between 1829 and 1834, all the Aboriginal people in Tasmania who had survived the state's martial law (which gave soldiers the right to arrest or shoot any Aboriginal person found in a settled area) were brought to the island. Of the 135 people who were transported to Wybalenna (meaning 'Black Man's House') to be 'civilised and educated', only forty-seven survived.

You can learn more about this sad story at the Wybalenna Historic Site, which was returned to the Aboriginal com-

munity in 1999. The chapel, cemetery and a homestead remain on the site. Other sites of interest here are Lillies Beach, where the stumps of the original wharf still stand, and Port Davies.

Today, a number of nearby islands have been returned to the Aboriginal community, including Big Dog Island, which is the focal point for the annual mutton-bird (*yolla* or moon bird) season, which lasts from September/October to April.

The business of catching, skinning and packing mutton birds has enormous importance for the local Aboriginal community. Mutton birds return from their migratory journey as far north as the Arctic Circle in September each year. Here they nest, looking after their chicks until mid-April, when they depart again on their long journey north. They leave the chicks to fend for themselves, and it is these

WHERE
Flinders Island is in Bass Strait, between Tasmania and Victoria.

WHEN
The best times to visit are during the mutton-bird season (from September/October to April) or during the Wybalenna Festival (January), when a stage is set up for musicians, traditional foods are cooked, and artists sell their work.

HOW
You can fly to Flinders Island with Airlines of Tasmania (03-6359 2312, 1800 144 460) from Moorabbin Airport, Melbourne, or Launceston, Tasmania. There's also a Southern Shipping Company ferry (03-6356 1753) from Bridport in Tasmania's northeast.

The Flinders Island Aboriginal Association Inc (FIAAI; 03-6359 3532) is in Lady Barron.

Wybalenna Chapel: one of the last poignant remnants of the Tasmanian Aboriginal settlement Photo: Geoffrey Lea/Auscape

chicks that are the target of the birders (mutton-bird hunters). Many people return from far afield to take part in the annual ritual, which has taken place for thousands of years and is a time of cultural renewal.

You can go over to Big Dog Island (a short trip from Lady Barron, at the southern end of Flinders Island) to see the birders at work in the shed run by the Flinders Island Aboriginal Association Inc (FIAAI), but you must get permission from the shed boss first by contacting the FIAAI.

You can't visit Big Dog outside the season, but you can pay a visit to the museum at Emita, near Wybalenna. It has a replica birding shed that gives you a feel for the industry as it was in the early days.

A Bass Srait short-tailed shearwater (muttonbird)
Photo: Graham Robertson/Auscape

The seashore at Marrawah, painted pink at sundown **Photo:** Gareth McCormack

Windswept Heritage:
North & West Coast Tasmania

The wild Southern Ocean hits the northwest corner of Tasmania in a dramatic confluence of wind, rock and spray, occasionally throwing up the remains of wrecked ships. At Marrawah the beaches and rocky outcrops can be hauntingly beautiful, particularly at dusk, and the seas are often huge.

While this rugged and remote region has seen minimal disturbance from European development, there are strong reminders of the region's long Aboriginal history, and some areas have now been proclaimed reserves to protect the relics, including rock carvings, middens and hut depressions.

There's a significant Aboriginal site along the road to Arthur River at West Point, and another beyond the township at Sundown Point, the latter with several dozen mudstone slabs engraved with mainly circular motifs. There are also

important traditional sites in the Arthur Pieman Conservation Area further south, and several impressive cave sites at Rocky Cape National Park (known to indigenous people as Tang Dim Mer) to the east.

But arguably the most important Aboriginal art site in the area, if not the state, is to be found seven kilometres north of Marrawah at Preminghana (formerly known as Mount Cameron West). Here you'll find low-lying slabs of rock encrusted with geometric motifs that are believed to date back at least two millennia. Also in this area are remnants of stone tools, the quarries from which these were dug, and middens. It's best to organise a guide to show you around.

Heading east, you can take in some important museums. In Devonport, there's the Tiagarra Aboriginal Culture Centre and Museum. Tiagarra means 'keep' and this museum has

WHERE
Marrawah is in the north-west corner of Tasmania, Devonport, Launceston and Deloraine are in the mid-north.

WHEN
The most popular time to visit Tassie is in summer and early autumn (December to March).

HOW
The Tasmanian Aboriginal Land Council (03-6231 0288) in North Hobart keeps a list of heritage officers who can take you to important sites.

The Tasmanian Aboriginal Corporation for Women's Arts and Crafts (03-6334 9378) is in Launceston.

Near Deloraine, Jahadi Indigenous Tours (03-6363 6172) offers tailored trips throughout the state, emphasising the beauty of Tasmania's wilderness and offering insights into Aboriginal culture and history.

Tiagarra (03-6424 8250) in Devonport offers guided tours if you book in advance.

Below, from top: Granville locals having a beer or two **Photo:** Oliver Strewe; Lichen-splattered rocks at Rocky Cape National Park near Wynyard **Photo:** Chris Mellor

over 2000 artefacts to give you an insight into local traditional culture. A walking track around the centre takes in significant rock engravings and there's a café and shop here selling Aboriginal arts and crafts.

In Launceston, the Queen Victoria Museum and Art Gallery has an exhibition on the Palawa (Tasmanian Aboriginal) community. The museum's collection includes beautiful *maireeners* (shell necklaces), bull-kelp water-carriers and throwing sticks. You can also see and purchase these traditional artworks at the Tasmanian Aboriginal Corporation for Women's Arts and Crafts (TACWAC).

There's plenty of adventure to be had in this region, including kayaking, bushwalking in old-growth rainforest and canoeing. If you prefer a slower pace you can call in at Yytambar Gallery to meet community artists over billy tea and damper (bush bread cooked on an open fire).

The psychedelic swoop of the Painted Cliffs, Maria Island Photo: Rob Blakers

The Oyster Bay Tribe: East Coast Tasmania

Stunning Wineglass Bay has been described as one of the world's most beautiful beaches. It's in Freycinet National Park, sheltered by the spectacular 300-metre-high pink-granite outcrops known as the Hazards.

The park is famous for its magnificent scenery, coastal heaths, orchids and other wildflowers. The local fauna includes black cockatoos, yellow wattlebirds, yellow-throated honeyeaters and Bennett's wallabies.

Here you can pitch your tent in the same area that was used as a winter camp by members of the Oyster Bay Tribe for thousands of years. The area is rich in shellfish and the large middens along Richardsons Beach, just one and a half kilometres into the park, are one of the signs of Aboriginal occupation. There are also many middens along the walk to Hazards Beach.

For more great views, head over to Waterloo Point in nearby Swansea. The Loontitetermairrelehoiner Aboriginal Heritage Walk wraps around the headland behind the golf course. It passes middens and interpretive boards that explain a little about Aboriginal history. The walk is named after the band of the Oyster Bay Tribe that once lived in the area. During mutton-bird season (from September/October to April) you can see the inhabitants return to their burrows at dusk.

If you're heading north, stop in at the St Helens History Room, which has displays on the North East Tribe with artefacts that you can handle, including ochre stones, grinding stones, flint blades (like those used for scarification) and a good collection of reference material. The Bay of Fires, nearby, was named by early European explorers after the Aboriginal fires they spotted along the coastline.

Evening light casts a warm glow over the Freycinet National Park **Photo:** Wes Walker

If you're going south, head to the town of Snug, south of Hobart. Here you'll find Oyster Cove, which was the destination for the forty-seven Tasmanian Aborigines who survived Wybalenna on Flinders Island (p34). In 1995, Oyster Cove was returned to the Tasmanian Aboriginal community and can now be visited independently. The best time to go is during the Oyster Cove Festival in mid-January.

The famous Aboriginal negotiator Truganini was born on Bruny Island, south of Snug. Mount Mangana on South Bruny is named after Truganini's father, who was a leader of the Nuennone Band of the South East Tribe.

The world's your oyster: oyster farmer with his produce **Photo:** Michael Gebicki

WHERE
Freycinet National Park is midway up the east coast of Tasmania. St Helens is on the northeast coast and Snug and Bruny Island are south of Hobart.

WHEN
From December to March is the most popular time to visit Tassie and if you're in Snug on the Saturday closest to 16 January, you can catch the Oyster Cove Festival. It's the state's biggest indigenous celebration and features musicians, artists and the sale of Aboriginal arts and crafts and food.

HOW
The Tasmanian Aboriginal Land Council (03-6231 0288) in North Hobart keeps a list of heritage officers who can take you to important sites.

St Helens History Room (03-6376 1744) in St Helens may also have information about local guides.

Weather-hollowed granite boulders hang in there at Remarkable Rocks Photo: Manfred Gottschalk

Weaving Magic:
The Coorong

The Coorong, a complex series of sand dunes and saltpans separated from the sea by the Younghusband Peninsula, takes its name from the Ngarrindjeri word *kurangh*, meaning 'long neck' (a reference to the very thin peninsula). According to the Ngarrindjeri, their Dreaming ancestor, Ngurundjeri, created the Coorong and the Murray River. A mighty wind blows off the Southern Ocean along the moody dunes of Ninety Mile Beach, in a landscape made famous by the movie *Storm Boy*.

This region provides the perfect habitat for the fresh-water rushes used for basket weaving. The Boandik of the southeast coast and the Ngarrindjeri of the Coorong are among the most celebrated weavers in Aboriginal Australia, renowned for their distinctive spiral designs and 'sister baskets' (so named because they're made up of two identical halves). Traditionally, weaving was used to make

baskets, mats, fish traps and other items to keep out the cold winds.

You can learn the ancient skill from the experts at Camp Coorong. At this wonderful cultural centre, Ngarrindjeri women teach basket weaving, and you can join a field trip with Ngarrindjeri Elders to see stone fish traps and visit the Raukkan Aboriginal community at Point McLeay, home of the church printed on Australia's fifty-dollar note.

You can stay at Camp Coorong's cabins or pitch a tent, and there's also a compact museum here with artefacts from the Coorong, locally made crafts (particularly baskets) and some items about Ngarrindjeri heritage.

Stop in at the nearby Coorong Wilderness Lodge for lunch and the chance to sample local bush tucker, such as Murray cod.

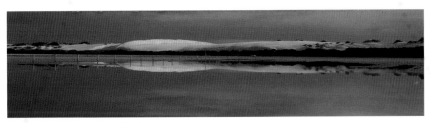

Marker posts and dunes at Tea Tree Crossing Photo: Diana Mayfield

Further south, visit the Lady Nelson Visitor & Discovery Centre in Mount Gambier, an impressive tourist office-cum-museum that boasts a reconstructed midden; an explanation about the Dreaming ancestor Craitbul (who created the nearby volcanoes); a marvellous audiovisual display about Christina Smith (a nineteenth-century Scottish woman who worked with the Boandik); and information about, and replicas of, cave rock art. While in Mount Gambier you can also stock up on Aboriginal art at the Cockatoo Dreaming Gallery.

Sculpted sand dunes, Younghusband Peninsula
Photo: Jason Edwards

WHERE
The Coorong is a narrow lagoon curving along the coast for 145 kilometres from Lake Alexandrina almost to Kingston South East, South Australia.

WHEN
Summer (December to February) is the most popular time to visit the Coorong, particularly during the Christmas and January school holidays; Easter is also a popular time.

HOW
Camp Coorong (08-8575 1557) is run by the Ngarrindjeri Lands and Progress Association.

Coorong Wilderness Lodge (08-8575 6001) is south of Meningie.

Lady Nelson Visitor & Discovery Centre (1800 087 187, 08-8724 9750) is in Mount Gambier.

Cockatoo Dreaming Gallery (08-8725 6200) is in Mount Gambier.

Adelaide Sightseeing (08-8231 4144) in Adelaide offers two of the better Coorong cruises. They include guided walks and lots of information about the region, including aspects of the resident Ngarrindjeri Aboriginal communities.

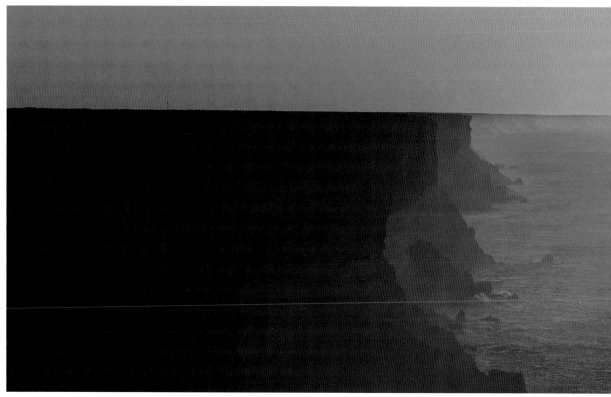

The precipitous edge of the Great Australian Bight at sunrise Photo: Richard I'Anson

From Outback to Sea: South Coast WA

The area along the coast south of Perth, curving east and heading towards the desert of the Nullarbor, is rich with indigenous history. Contrast defines this route: caves and scrub in Yallingup, the power of solid grey granite landscape in Albany, the vastness of the Eyre Highway.

Yallingup (p44) is a tiny settlement near Margaret River, surrounded by surf mist, coves and deep olive green coastal vegetation.

Round the bend of Australia's southwesternmost corner and you'll be on its southern coast. Albany (formerly Kincinnup), the oldest European settlement in the state, was established in 1826 and is now the bustling commercial centre of Western Australia's southern region. The King George Sound area, now a mecca for divers, was occupied by the Minang Nyoongar people long before Europeans arrived. There is

much evidence of their presence, especially around Oyster Harbour's northern shore, where the remains of fish traps recorded in 1791 by Captain Vancouver (the first European to discover this area) can still be seen at low tide. The traps, which were crescent shaped and up to 100 metres long, were made of boughs and cross-sticks, with a low stone wall along the bottom to stop the fish escaping. Early white visitors were amazed at the large quantities of fish caught in such traps.

The pristine town of Esperance, smack bang in the middle of some of Australia's most magnificent coastline, is a great place to stop. World-class beaches, national parks and the spectacular Bay of Isles create an idyllic picture. From here it's an easy 202-kilometre run up into the outback.

From the hard-baked town of Norseman, 200 kilometres north of Esperance, you can begin the intrepid trek across

42

Coastal flora on the rocks at Torndirrup National Park, near Albany **Photo:** Rob Blakers

the Eyre Highway, which crosses the southern edge of the vast Nullarbor Plain (p106). Between Balladonia and Caiguna lies the famous 90 Mile Straight; at 145 kilometres, this is one of the longest stretches of straight road in the world – the perilous line over which the outback staggers to become sea.

Some ten kilometres south of Caiguna is a memorial to John Baxter, explorer Edward John Eyre's companion. Baxter was killed in 1841 by two of three Aboriginal guides who mutinied because of lack of water and supplies on the journey. So it was only Eyre and Wylie, Eyre's young Aboriginal guide, who arrived in Albany after four and a half months, having survived on bush craft. Eyre once described the Nullarbor as 'the sort of place one gets into in bad dreams'. No kidding.

Venture southeast of Cocklebiddy for the Eyre Bird Observatory. Housed in the Eyre Telegraph Station in the Nuytsland Nature Reserve, it's one of the best places in the country for bird-watching. Species you'll encounter include Major Mitchell (pink) cockatoos, mallee fowl, bronzewings, honeyeaters, waders and terns, and regular activities and courses are also held here. Otherwise, as you drive you'll see many birds of prey – including the incredible wedge-tailed eagle, with its two-metre wingspan – hunching over road kills along all sections of the highway.

Postmen beware: letterbox on the Albany road **Photo:** Peter Ptschelinzew

WHERE
The southern coast of Western Australia includes over 2000 kilometres of vast and various beauty.

WHEN
If you're heading inland, don't even consider travelling from November to March, when the heat is extreme, or after heavy rain. From July to October is whale-watching season in Albany, when southern right whales can often be spotted near King George Sound.

HOW
This route assumes you're zipping along in a car – Western Australia is big no matter which bit you're in. For the outback section your vehicle should be a four-wheel drive. Otherwise, given that the Eyre is the most important transcontinental route in Australia, there are daily scheduled bus services on the Perth–Adelaide route with Greyhound Australia. There's also a rail option, one of the great railway journeys of the world, the *Indian Pacific*.

In Albany, the regional office of the Department of Indigenous Affairs (08-9842 3000) is a good source of information for Nyoongar tourism-based ventures.

Grass trees fan delicately out, capturing the sun's rays, Dryandra Reserve Photo: Minden Pictures/APL

Tuck into the Southwest: Margaret River Area

The lush southwestern corner of Western Australia is the stuff of summer holidays at the beach – surfing, dolphin spotting and winery tours. There are lots of gourmet treats to try – everything from a sharp cheddar to a bardi-grub (beetle larvae) pâté. In fact, this area offers a superb opportunity to sample bush tucker and learn more about traditional food.

At Yallingup, a stop at the Wardan Aboriginal Centre is a must. There are lots of activities on offer, including a bush-story trail, detailing bush tucker and medicine; spear-throwing workshops; a gallery; and regular performances. Nearby is the Ngilgi Cave of Aboriginal legend, a wonderland of stalag-mites and stalactites, named after Ngilgi (a good warrior spirit). During the Creation Time (Tjukurpa), the cave was inhabited by an evil spirit named Wolgine. Concerned for the safety of his people, Ngilgi decided to rid the cave of

the bad spirit. In the violent battle that ensued, part of the cave collapsed and Wolgine was driven up through the earth and banished, allowing Ngilgi to claim the cave as his own.

South of Yallingup lies the town of Margaret River, whose ample attractions – top surf, undulating bushland, some of Australia's best wineries – have made it one of Western Australia's most popular destinations. One fascinating tour is the search for forest secrets with Bushtucker Tours' Cave & Canoe Tour. It combines walking and canoeing up the Margaret River, and delves into aspects of Aboriginal cul-ture, such as uses of flora and bush-tucker tastings, before ending with a descent into an adventure cave.

Heading inland, about 160 kilometres southeast of Perth, Dryandra Forest is a rare haven for thirteen of the mammal species that once formed part of the traditional Nyoongar

Tourist drive 250 explores the stunning coast south of Yallingup Photo: Chris Mellor

Looking after the big cheeses at Margaret River Photo: John Hay

diet. The Nyoongars mainly lived here during the wetter months, when food and water were abundant, then retreated to coastal areas such as Mandurah (now a popular beach resort), seventy-four kilometres south of Perth, to see out the hot, dry summer.

There are several cultural sites in the reserve and you can visit one of them – a small red-ochre mine – on the Ochre Trail. A handful of information signs en route tell you a little of the forest's Aboriginal heritage.

South of here, in Kojonup, the Kodja Place is a modern interpretation centre with displays on the local Aboriginal and Wadjela (nonindigenous) communities. Highlights include the Kodja Gallery, where Nyoongar guides will introduce you to local culture and artworks, and the Story Place, with accounts of the Stolen Generations.

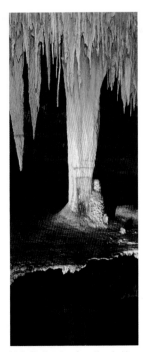

Icicle-like limestone formations inside Lake Cave Photo: Wayne Walton

WHERE
This region is in the south-western corner of Western Australia.

WHEN
The area is most popular in summer (December to February), but come at the end of October for the Back to Pinjarra Day festival, held in the town of Pinjarra, on the banks of the Murray River, eighty kilometres south of Perth. It commemorates the Pinjarra Massacre of 1834, when Governor James Stirling, backed up by twenty-five whites including police and soldiers, opened fire on a group of around seventy Nyoongar people, breaking Aboriginal resistance to colonisation in the area. The festival is a celebration of survival and includes story-telling, dance performances, theatre, bands and arts and crafts stalls.

HOW
Wardan Aboriginal Centre (08-9756 6566) is near Yallingup. The Kodja Place Visitor & Interpretive Centre (08-9831 0500) is in Kojonup.

You can take a cultural awareness tour of Ngilgi Cave with Mitch Hutchins, the granddaughter of a Wardandi Nyoongar Elder. She talks about a wide range of topics, including totemic ancestors, Nyoongar contemporary history, law, spirituality, family values and bushcraft. Book with Waljin Consultancies on 08-9756 2075.

Bushtucker Tours' Cave & Canoe Tour (08-9757 9084) is based in the tiny seaside retreat of Prevelly Park, near Margaret River.

Bush Tucker & Medicine

The seemingly stark Australian landscape is like one giant supermarket for those in the know. Australia's bush tucker and bush medicines have sustained indigenous communities for thousands of years. Many Aboriginal Australians still eat traditional foods and prepare traditional remedies, well aware of their health-giving properties.

Bush tucker varies according to the country's particular regions and seasons. The diet of indigenous groups living along Australia's coastline, for instance, differs from that of groups living in desert areas or tropical regions. Common to all communities is the conscious manner in which food is gathered: they only take what's needed and never pull up anything by the roots, except for edible tubers. This ensures that edible plants and game can regenerate. Fresh water from rivers, lakes and springs is also vital and, for Aborigines in desert areas, knowing the locations of springs, water holes and natural wells is a matter of survival.

Traditionally, indigenous groups living along Australia's vast coast subsisted on marine animals (fish, shellfish, crabs and turtles), roots, fruit, small game and reptiles, which varied in species from region to region. Depending on the area, freshwater crustaceans such as marron (a large fresh-water crayfish) and *jilgies* (the Western Australian name for yabbies, or crayfish) may have been available. In the Torres Strait Islands, communities also ate dugong (a relative of the manatee and walrus), while in the tropical north, *jinyp* (stingrays) were eaten. Some wildflowers such as grevillea and banksia were sucked for their sweetness, and the tips of the Western Australian orange Christmas trees were chewed as gum, as were wattle and manna gum.

Unlike the indigenous people of the mainland, Torres Strait Islanders traditionally derived much of their food from gardening. With their rich volcanic soil, the eastern islands were especially bountiful. Among the crops grown were yam, taro, banana and coconut.

The harsh desert climate made hunting and gathering more difficult. Food sources are scarcer in the desert and at times hunters had to travel great distances before they found any kangaroos or emus. Other game included snakes, small lizards and the larger *bungarras* (the Yamatji name for goannas). In the desert regions, game was thrown on a campfire and cooked whole. Vegetables were either cooked in coals or eaten raw, such as yams or *cunmanggu* (wild potatoes), which taste like sweet potatoes. *Wamulu* (bush

tomatoes), *minyarra* (wild onions), honey, wild grain and seeds from the woolly butt tree (which are crushed and made into a flour for damper, a bush bread cooked in hot ashes) were also collected. If the rivers and creeks had permanent water holes, fish such as mullet and bream were added to the menu.

Communities in the tropical northern parts of Australia enjoy a totally different lifestyle from that of the desert peoples and communities further south. The Kimberley (at Western Australia's top end), the Northern Territory and Far North Queensland have areas of lush growth and tropical downpours. These areas have two major seasons: Wet and Dry. During the cyclonic Wet, huge areas of land are subject to flooding and plant and animal life thrives. The rivers and lagoons supply *cherrabun* (the Kimberley word for yabbies), mussels, catfish, barramundi, turtles, crocodiles and wild ducks. Edible water reeds or rushes grow in lakes and swamps, while the land offers a plentiful supply of meat, including *barni* (goanna), *gunanunja* (emu), *bingajuooi* (wild turkey), *niminburr* (flying fox), kangaroo and snake. Snack foods come in the form of *nyilli nyilli* (bush bubblegum), *mukabala* (bush banana), wild passionfruit, *lulguoi* (boab nut), *kilu* (wild tomato), bush honey and flowers from the *jigul* tree.

In the inland nondesert areas, such as the Nyoongar people's territory in south and southwestern Western Australia, there are six distinct climatic changes. The Nyoongar gauge the season by the food sources that are available. Traditionally, inland communities foraged for insects such as bardi grubs (found in wattle and grass trees); birds, including rosellas and ducks; reptiles (snakes and various lizards); and mammals, including *yongka* (kangaroos), *waitj* (emus) and *coomarl* (possums). They also ate a variety of fruits, flowers, berries and nuts, and collected various seeds that were ground and mixed with water before being baked in coals to make damper or eaten as a paste.

Many plants and trees in the Australian bush also make good medicine. Aboriginal Australians who have lived off their own lands are familiar with the medicinal properties of many plants. Bush medicines are mostly used as inhalants, antiseptics and liniments. For coughs, headaches and a runny nose, the young leaf tips of paperbark trees are crushed in the hands and inhaled. The bark from red river gums provides a powerful antiseptic: the bark is boiled and, when cool, rubbed on sore or irritated skin. Indigenous Australians have adopted thousands of such herbal remedies, with some using up to twenty ingredients.

Drumming up a good time at the Fremantle Festival, held annually in November Photo: Peter Ptschelinzew

Colonial Clashes: Rottnest Island

'Rotto', as Rottnest Island is known by the locals, is a sandy island with turquoise waters and secluded white-sand beaches. You can swim, dive or snorkel in crystal-clear water among shipwrecks and some of the southernmost coral in the world, or just rent a bike and track down some quokkas.

But Rottnest Island also has a starring role to play in the brutal history of colonisation, and you'll appreciate today's laid-back atmosphere even more when you contrast it with the island's grim past.

Rotto (known to Nyoongars as Wadjemup) was a prison for Aboriginal males from all over Western Australia from 1838 to 1931. About 3700 men and boys were imprisoned here in that time, often for such crimes as cattle-spearing and petty theft, but also for being 'troublemakers'. The prison-

ers were poorly clothed and fed, kept in grossly overcrowded cells, and made to perform hard labour such as quarrying and building work. Over 370 prisoners died on Rottnest, mostly from disease; sixty succumbed to an influenza epidemic in 1883.

You can visit the excellent Rottnest Museum, built by Aboriginal prisoners in 1857, to learn more about its history of incarceration, as well as about local shipwrecks and the island's natural history. There are also many guided tours around Rotto, including an Aboriginal Historical Walk that takes in the sacred site of the Wadjemup Aboriginal Cemetery. Ask at the visitors centre for details.

Over on the mainland, the Fremantle Aboriginal Heritage Tour is a great opportunity to learn about the history of the region with an Aboriginal guide. It introduces the Dreaming

Rottnest Island is bliss for lovers of water sports Photo: Peter Ptschelinzew

WHERE
Rottnest Island is about nineteen kilometres off the coast of Fremantle (Western Australia), Perth's port.

WHEN
Rottnest Island is wildly popular in summer (December to February) and during school holidays, when ferries and accommodation are booked out months in advance. Be sure to plan ahead or visit in the off season.

HOW
Frequent boats travel to Rotto from Fremantle and Perth.

Rottnest Island Visitor Centre (08-9372 9732) is in the Thomson Bay Settlement at the end of the main jetty.

The Fremantle Aboriginal Heritage Tour departs from the Western Australian Maritime Museum – book through Greg Nannup (0405 630 606).

The Round House, Western Australia's oldest public building, is on Arthur Head in Fremantle.

tracks that run under the sea from the mainland to beyond Wadjemup (Rottnest Island). To the Nyoongar people, Wadjemup was believed to be the home of spirits.

Also on the tour, you'll visit Fremantle's Round House, a sacred site for the Nyoongar people, in which Aboriginal prisoners were held in appalling conditions before they were taken to Rottnest Island. You'll hear about a deadly curse placed on CY O'Connor by the Nyoongar; as the engineer-in-charge of the Fremantle port project that destroyed a Nyoongar river crossing, O'Connor was held responsible for the major disruption this caused in the pattern of Nyoongar life. Not long after, O'Connor killed himself. Not surprisingly, the Nyoongar have their own theory as to why this happened. And you'll learn of the tragedy of Yagan, a Nyoongar resistance fighter whose head was cut off, smoked, decorated and taken to England as an exhibit.

The quokka, found only on Rottnest Island Photo: Dennis Jones

A red wattlebird enjoys a drink of kangaroo paw nectar **Photo:** Chris Mellor

Wildflower Wilderness:
Walyunga & Yanchep National Parks

With lovely walking trails, sensational wildflowers, and plenty of wildlife to keep you company, these two parks are very popular day trips from Perth. They're also great places to deepen your understanding of traditional Nyoongar life.

The beautiful Swan River, a continuation of the Avon River, which flows just east of the park in the scenic Avon Valley, cuts a narrow gorge through Walyunga National Park, creating a series of pretty pools in summer and a raging torrent for white-water rafters in winter.

The park contains the largest-known Aboriginal camp sites of the Nyoongar people, which were still in use last century. Thanks to its abundant food resources, this area was an important ceremonial meeting place for Nyoongar clans from as far away as York and the Moore River. The site,

which has been used for more than 6000 years, also had good deposits of chert and quartz suitable for making tools. These were created by a Wagyl spirit (huge Serpent Ancestor), which shaped the river and land in this area.

The Aboriginal Heritage Trail is a pretty walk along the west bank of the Avon River between Walyunga and Boongarup Pools. Information signs en route introduce you to the traditional uses of local plants and animals, as well as a couple of the area's spirit entities. These include the evil Warrdarchi – hairy little creatures that catch swimmers and steal babies who cry in the night!

Nearby at Henley Brook you can drop into Maali Mia, an Aboriginal-owned arts and crafts gallery that holds cultural evenings with bush-tucker tastings and storytelling from September to May.

WHERE
Walyunga National Park is forty kilometres (one hour's drive) northeast of Perth, Western Australia. Yanchep National Park is fifty kilometres north of Perth.

WHEN
Spring (September to November) is the best time to visit the parks if you're a fan of wildflowers. The Avon Descent Race, Western Australia's premier white-water event, is a gruelling two-day race that takes place in Walyunga National Park each August.

HOW
Maali Mia (08-9296 0704) is in Henley Brook.

Further to the west, Yanchep is one of Western Australia's oldest national parks, a landscape of tuart (a type of eucalypt) and banksia woodlands, beautiful wetlands and limestone caves. In times past, this was an important ceremonial meeting place for Nyoongar people living between the Swan and Moore Rivers.

Here you can join an Aboriginal guide for a tour through the village of Wangi Mia (meaning 'the talking place'). You'll learn about traditional skills such as how traditional shelters were constructed, how the family fire was sited, and the manufacture and uses of *bigo* (an Araldite-like cement made from dried kangaroo dung, charcoal and grass-tree resin). Another highlight is the 'Didgeridoo and Dance' performance, where you can pick up some Nyoongar dancing techniques and learn about the didge.

You can also walk the Dwerta Mia Walking Trail through a spooky collapsed cave system, or meet Australia's largest colony of koalas. There's a stunning wildflower garden here, too.

The Yaberoo Budjara Heritage Trail links Yanchep National Park with Lake Joondalup in the south. It follows a chain of lakes that provided a major source of food and water for the Nyoongar.

Below, from top: Golden bandicoot encounters some well-travelled hiking boots Photo: Mitch Reardon; Pretty purple mulla mulla Photo: John Banagan

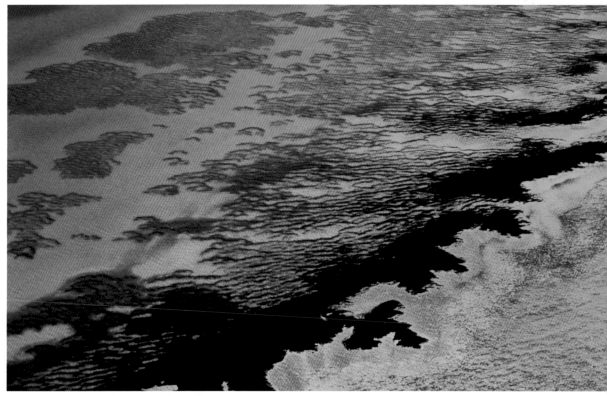

The intensely turquoise waters of Shark Bay Photo: Richard I'Anson

Wildlife Wonderland: Shark Bay Area

Monkey Mia's famous bottlenose dolphins have made Shark Bay Marine Park famous all around the world. They turn up in the crystal-clear, aquamarine shallows like clockwork every day and are so popular that the morning feeding session can be a bit of a circus!

You can also join tours here to see dugongs, turtles and, in summer, tiger sharks and sea snakes – and this can be more rewarding than jostling in the crowds to see the dolphins.

The abundant wildlife on land and sea in this area made the living easy for the saltwater Yamatji of the Nganda and Malgana tribes. Shark Bay was also the site of the first recorded landing by a European on Australian soil. Dutch explorer Dirk Hartog anchored at the island that now bears his name in 1616, just off Denham – Shark Bay's main town.

The Monkey Mia resort runs Aboriginal cultural tours; an Aboriginal guide will take you along a foreshore trail to learn some Yamatji survival skills, such as how to find bush tucker and bush medicine and how to identify animal tracks around Shark Bay (known to Aboriginal people as Gadhaagudu, which means 'two bays').

Another fine stroll is the interesting Boolbardi walk, running along the shore from Denham to the Town Bluff. The two rows of curved rocks here are believed to be an Aboriginal fish trap.

About four kilometres west of Denham, François Péron National Park is well worth a stop for its untouched beaches, dramatic cliffs, salt lakes and rare marsupial species, such as bilbies, rufous-hare wallabies and western-barred bandicoots. There's a visitors centre at the old Peron homestead, six kilometres from the main road, where a former artesian

The long straight road to Denham Photo: Richard l'Anson

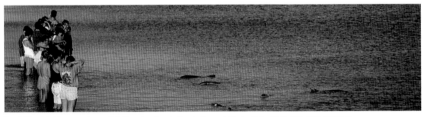

Inquisitive dolphins come to greet visitors standing in the shallows at Monkey Mia Photo: Peter Ptschelinzew

WHERE
Shark Bay (850 kilometres north of Perth) and Monkey Mia (twenty-five kilometres northeast Denham) are in Western Australia.

WHEN
The area can get uncomfortably hot in summer (December to February). The best time to visit is between April and October, when winds are light and temperatures pleasant.

HOW
The Monkey Mia Dolphin Resort (1800 653 611, 08-9948 1320) runs Aboriginal cultural walks.

The New Vision Gallery Shop (08-9941 3555) is in Carnarvon.

bore has been converted to a soothing thirty-five-degree Celsius hot tub – one of the more novel spots for a sunset soak!

Péron is the subject of Australia's largest and most ambitious ecosystem regeneration programme, Project Eden. Run by the Department of Conservation & Land Management (CALM), the project is attempting to eradicate feral animals, re-establish populations of endemic species and develop techniques that can be applied to other degraded arid zones in Australia. The key has been the isolation of the peninsula from mainland Australia with an electric fence at the isthmus. There are plans to upgrade the access road to François Péron National Park and set up night-viewing positions for wildlife-spotting.

Some 330 kilometres north of Péron in Carnarvon is a strong indigenous community and the New Vision Gallery Shop, where you can buy paintings, sculptures and emu eggs.

A well-fed pelican lazes at Monkey Mia
Photo: John Banagan

Cath and Deb catch the last rays **Photo:** Peter Solness

Pearl Luggers: Broome

Perched on the edge of the Indian Ocean, a thousand miles from anywhere, Broome was once a wild frontier outpost, the pearling capital of the world and arguably one of the most unique places in Australia. Today it's a popular travel destination that trades on its colourful history, stunning coast and multicultural mix.

It's not hard to fall for Broome's easy-going tropical charms – especially when you're lying on the sand at Cable Beach or settling back in a deckchair under the stars to watch a movie at Sun Pictures. It's a perfect base from which to explore the rugged wilderness of the Kimberley and the coastline and Aboriginal communities of the Dampier Peninsula (p58).

The Aboriginal name for the Broome region is Goolarri and about a quarter of its population belongs to one of five local language groups: Yawura, Bardi, Nyul Nyul, Nimanburr and Jukun.

Local Aborigines collected pearl shell for ceremonies and ornamentation long before Broome became a pearling centre in the 1870s. In the early days of the industry, many Aborigines were forced to work on pearl luggers in virtual slave conditions, and Aboriginal women were the most highly prized divers.

Before long Broome began to attract Chinese traders, Japanese, Malay, Filipino and Koepanger (Timorese) divers, developing into an oriental shantytown run by European pearling masters. The town's multicultural make-up is the legacy of this era, when 400 pearl luggers worked the waters out of Broome. Pearl farms have now replaced open-sea diving.

A turquoise timber door to Broome's past **Photo:** John Hay

You can get a taste of Broome's pearling past at the Pearl Luggers display centre with its two restored boats, extensive memorabilia and tours run by former divers. The Japanese cemetery, which has a small Aboriginal section, is a testimony to the perils of pearling.

The Manbana aquaculture centre focuses on Aboriginal peoples' connection to the sea, their participation in the pearling industry and traditional fishing practices. It's also a working aquaculture hatchery spawning trochus (conical-shaped molluscs), prawns and aquarium fish.

To soak up the town's history, take a stroll around Old Broome (also known as Chinatown). This was once a rough-and-tumble mix of pearl sheds, saloons, opium dens, billiard halls and brothels. Today it's the town's retail and entertainment hub, offering some big-city creature comforts and plenty of attractive Asian-influenced colonial architecture.

For nine decades, the open-air cinema Sun Pictures has brought a Hollywood sheen to the dusty outback. Nothing beats hunkering down in a deckchair in the heart of Chinatown and watching the big screen under a tropical night sky.

Above, from top: Cath and Deb warm up to Broome
Photos: Michael Hutchinson (top, centre and bottom); Peter Solness

Open for business at the Sun Pictures open-air cinema **Photo:** Michael Hutchinson/Short Street Gallery

Resting in peace at the Japanese Cemetery **Photo:** Michael Hutchinson/Short Street Gallery

If you're lucky enough to be in Broome on a cloudless night when a full moon rises, take a stroll down to Town Beach, where the reflections of the moon off the rippling mud flats in Roebuck Bay create a wonderful golden effect known as the Staircase to the Moon. An evening market on the beach adds to the lively atmosphere.

Town Beach is a great spot for a swim at high tide during the day, but the most popular spot to lie back and let it all wash over you is Cable Beach. With Broome's signature white sand and turquoise water, it's justifiably one of the most famous beaches in Australia.

For some folk, a camel ride along Cable Beach at sunset is almost compulsory. It's a leisurely stroll aimed squarely at tourists, but camel trains run by Afghan cameleers did once service large parts of the Kimberley, moving goods through

terrain too rough for horses. A more relaxing Broome ritual is sundowner cocktails at the beautiful Cable Beach Club right on the foreshore.

If you want to put Aboriginal and European habitation of the area into perspective, cruise down to Gantheaume Point at the southern tip of Cable Beach. The gorgeous red cliffs here have been eroded into surreal shapes and, at extremely low tide, 120-million-year-old dinosaur tracks are visible.

WHERE
Broome is 2250 kilometres
northeast of Perth, Western
Australia.

WHEN
Peak season is the Dry,
between April and Septem-
ber. One of the busiest and
best times to visit is during
Shinju Matsuri (Festival
of the Pearl) – a ten-day
festival held in August/
September that commemo-
rates Broome's early pearling years and multicultural
heritage. It features street
parades, the Shinju Ball
and dragon-boat races. The
Staircase to the Moon phe-
nomenon occurs between
March and October for only
three nights per month.
Markets are held on the
first two nights to coincide
with this event.

HOW
The Manbana aquaculture
centre (08-9192 3844),
in the port precinct, offers
one-hour guided tours.
A handful of operators
offer camel rides on
Cable Beach. The *Broome
Heritage Trail* brochure
details a self-guided stroll
around the town's historic
sights. It's available from
the Broome Visitors Centre
(08-9192 2222).

I love it up here. The country's beautiful, the weather's glorious and seeing the red earth and the blue water at Cable Beach is magnificent. It's a crossroads too. There are so many people here, from all walks of life, and there's a very accepting energy about the place. You can be the person you want to be in Broome. —Deb

The magnificent altar encrusted with pearl shells at Sacred Heart Church **Photo:** Michael Hutchinson

Famous Follies: Beagle Bay

The Dampier Peninsula is renowned for its unspoilt coast, remote Aboriginal communities and the sandy corrugated track running its length which has been called 'the second-worst road in Australia'. Driving north from Broome on this dodgy road will bring you to the sleepy Aboriginal community of Beagle Bay.

Pay a permit fee on arrival and you can drive through the community and visit the Sacred Heart Church – a striking white Spanish Mission–style building that's one of the most poignant symbols of the contact history between Aborigines and Europeans in northern Australia.

Its story begins with the arrival of French Trappist monks in Beagle Bay in 1890. They established a school and a refuge for local Aborigines from the brutalities of European pearlers and pastoralists. German Pallotines took over

their work in 1901 and were joined six years later by a feisty group of Irish nuns from the Sisters of St John of God.

At the outbreak of World War I, fearing internment, the German priests announced their intention to build a cathedral at Beagle Bay as a monument to peace. This ambitious folly was built by local Aborigines and constructed entirely of local material.

Over a four-year period, while Europe was engulfed in war, they made 60,000 bricks by hand and cemented them together using mortar made from cockle shells to turn the Sacred Heart Church into a reality.

In the ensuing decades, thousands of Aboriginal children from across the Kimberley who were removed from their

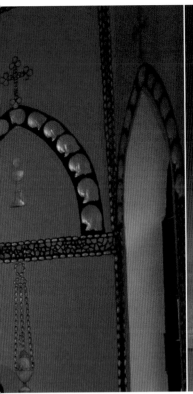

I think the curtain's been drawn back for both of us. You can see how this country and the people are affecting Cath, in a very profound sense. And for both of us it's been medicine for the soul, it's changed a lot about who I am and where I want to go.

—Deb

WHERE
Beagle Bay is on the Dampier Peninsula, 118 kilometres north of Broome.

WHEN
The best time to visit is between April and September. At other times of year the road may be impassable.

HOW
The Dampier Peninsula is Aboriginal land. Once you reach the Beagle Bay Aboriginal community (08-9192 4913), you can't miss the church. The road to the community is rough as bags so you'll need a four-wheel drive and, unless you're on a tour, you'll need to be completely self-sufficient. Half a dozen companies in Broome offer four-wheel-drive tours or transport to the Dampier Peninsula, including visits to Beagle Bay. Pick up a copy of the *Dampier Peninsula Travellers Guide* from the Broome Visitors Centre (08-9192 2222), where you can check on the condition of the road, book tours and – absolutely essential – book accommodation in advance.

Deb cuddles up to the locals Photo: Michael Hutchinson

families by misguided government policies were raised and educated at the Beagle Bay Mission by the Irish sisters.

Now the tables have turned and the children who were brought up at the mission proudly run the community. Self-governing since the 1970s, they have invited the church to continue its work in Beagle Bay and run the local school.

Break the drive, take a pew and pay your respects at this extraordinary monument to human endeavour. The pearl-shell-encrusted altar is a sight to behold.

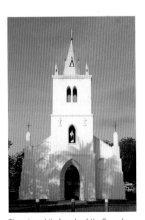

The crisp white façade of the Sacred Heart Church Photo: Michael Hutchinson

Cath goes for a run at low tide Photo: Michael Hutchinson

As Remote As It Gets:
Cape Leveque

Cape Leveque is a ridiculously scenic spot at the tip of the Dampier Peninsula – all pristine beaches, crystal-clear water, memorable sunsets and stunning red cliffs. If you want to get away from it all, this paradisaical spot – literally at the end of road – is as remote as you could ever hope to get.

Lorded over by a picturebook lighthouse, the cape is named after French hydrographer Pierre Lévêque, who sailed into the area aboard Nicolas Baudin's *Géographe* in 1803. Kooljaman is the Bardi name for the area.

Bardi people from the nearby communities of One Arm Point (p62) and Djarindjin have established the award-winning Kooljaman wilderness camp at Cape Leveque. It's become the poster child for sensitive, low-impact, indigenous-owned tourism in Western Australia.

Kooljaman camp is a spacious unhurried place built around the cape's lighthouse. It has a variety of accommodation, from safari tents on elevated decks with panoramic views of the ocean to modest bush cabins and a handful of basic-as-can-be palm-frond beach shelters right on the water's edge.

Most people are more than happy taking in the views, swimming, snorkelling and sunning themselves on the cape's beaches, but there's also dinghy hire, fantastic fishing at nearby Hunters Creek, whale-watching (between July and October when migrating humpback whales visit) and scenic flights over the outlying Buccaneer Archipelago (p62).

Layered rock formation Photo: Michael Hutchinson/Short Street Gallery

From left to right, The lighthouse at Cape Leveque, signalling since 1912 Photo: Michael Hutchinson; A stand of pandanus palms in the dunes Photo: Michael Hutchinson/Short Street Gallery

This country is spectacular. It makes me feel proud to be Australian and an indigenous one at that. — Cath

Cath and Deb share a laugh on the rocks
Photo: Michael Hutchinson

WHERE

Cape Leveque is 220 kilometres north of Broome at the tip of the Dampier Peninsula, in Western Australia.

WHEN

The Dry is between April and September. The road from Broome may be impassable at other times.

HOW

The drive from Broome to Cape Leveque takes about three hours on a bone-jarring corrugated sandy track. You'll need a four-wheel drive and should check road conditions at the Broome Visitors Centre (08-9192 2222) before setting off. Half a dozen companies in Broome offer four-wheel-drive tours or transport to the Dampier Peninsula, and virtually all visit Cape Leveque. If you're staying at Kooljaman wilderness camp, you can fly from Broome to the camp airstrip in just under an hour with King Leopold Air (08-9193 7155).

Kooljaman Cape Leveque (08-9192 4970) resort has a basic store and a restaurant open between April and October. The resort can arrange scenic flights, and mud-crabbing, bush-tucker and cultural tours with local indigenous guides.

Giving the girls a boomerang-throwing lesson **Photo:** Michael Hutchinson

Treacherous Tides: Sunday Island & the Buccaneer Archipelago

The 800-plus islands of the stunning Buccaneer Archipel-ago (also known as Thousand Islands) are part of a rugged submerged coastline that stretches north–east from the tip of the Dampier Peninsula to the Indian Ocean.

The archipelago is Bardi (or Jawi) country and used to be home to a small population of reef dwellers who gathered seafood and hunted dugong and turtle, using tidal move-ments to sail between the islands on mangrove rafts.

Indigenous groups, who have a vast knowledge of the tides, sea life and marine geography of the area, still visit traditional sites on the islands, even though they are now uninhabited.

The last settlement of any size in the archipelago was on the X-shaped Sunday Island – a picturesque spot with

small bays, white beaches, turquoise water and rugged red cliffs.

The settlement grew around an Anglican mission estab-lished on the island at the end of the nineteenth century by the son of an English peer. More than a hundred people lived on the island, whose economy was reliant on trading pearlshell and trepang (sea cucumber). The mission was abandoned in the 1950s and the Aboriginal population was encouraged to move to Derby, on a peninsula jutting into King Sound, where they lived in poor conditions, exiled from their country, on the edge of the salt flats.

In the late 1960s, after a decade of unease, an attempt was made to resettle the island, but this proved impractical and was abandoned in 1972 when authorities built a new settlement for the Sunday Island community at One Arm

Sand and water swirl around One Arm Point Photo: Michael Hutchinson

Point, at the northeastern tip of the Dampier Peninsula. The ruins of the mission and the remnants of past occupation, including abandoned houses and graves from the pearling era, can still be seen on Sunday Island today.

Sunday Island sits at the head of King Sound, which is home to some of the most treacherous tides in Australia. Whirlpools, surging riptides, reversible waterfalls, and ten-knot, eleven-metre tides make this no place for a novice to go exploring in a tinny (aluminium dinghy).

You can visit the resettled Sunday Island community at One Arm Point, which boasts a population of around 400 people, most of whom still live from the bounty of the sea.

Above left: Cath and Deb on the boat to Sunday Island
Above centre: Cath and Deb with a new friend
Above right: Deb dons a snorkel
Photos: Michael Hutchinson

WHERE
Sunday Island is in the King Sound, about ten kilometres northeast of One Arm Point, in Western Australia. One Arm Point is seventeen kilometres east of Cape Leveque, and approximately 240 kilometres northeast of Broome.

WHEN
The best time to visit is in the Dry, between April and September.

HOW
Goombading Cultural Scenic Tours runs day trips from Cape Leveque (p60) to Sunday Island that include reef-walking, snorkelling, fishing and a historic tour. Tours can be booked through the Kooljaman resort (08-9192 4970).

For an insight into the special connection the Bardi people here have with the sea, the Angus family runs Mundunn Tours (08-9192 4121), which offers fishing, oyster-collecting and mud-crabbing excursions in tidal creeks. You can also book a tour through the Kooljaman resort.

Not to be missed is a scenic flight over the Buccaneer Archipelago from Cape Leveque, Broome or Derby. Or, for a taste of life in Derby's remote communities and stations, join the mail run (a seven-hour flight) on Wednesday or Thursday. Contact the Derby Visitor Centre (08-9191 1426 or 1800 621 426) for information. If you want a closer look – and have a fistful of dollars – luxury cruises operate from Broome. Call the Broome Visitors Centre (08-9192 2222) for details.

Desert

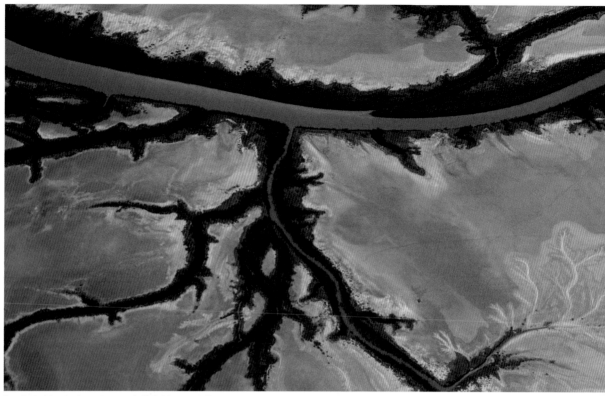

Down in the delta: the river system near the Gulf of Carpentaria **Photo:** Tony Wheeler

Rainforest to Savannah: Kennedy Hwy & the Gulf Developmental Rd

This route takes you from the rainforested hills outside Cairns to the drier country on the edge of the Great Dividing Range. It then travels across the vast savannah that extends all the way to the Gulf of Carpentaria.

Between Atherton and Ravenshoe (p196) the Kennedy Highway passes the eerie Mount Hypipamee crater. There's good bird-watching in this little rainforest park – watch out for the golden bowerbird as you walk the trails. It's a scenic walk past Dinner Falls to the narrow, 138-metre-deep crater with its moody lake, covered in a green crust of duckweed, far below. Back at Dinner Falls there's a welcome swimming area.

West of Ravenshoe are the Innot Hot Springs, where you can relax in hot mineral baths or dig your own hot pool in the river. Further on is the Forty Mile Scrub National Park,

an unusual dry rainforest. Just south of the park is the turn-off to the Gulf Developmental Road and the Undara Volcanic National Park.

Here at Undara, massive lava tubes were created around 190,000 years ago after a volcanic eruption. The extremely hot flow of lava continued for three months, creating these fascinating formations and the longest lava flow in the world at 160 kilometres.

Mount Surprise, a lively little township on the route of the historic *Savannahlander* train to Forsayth, lies fifty kilometres west of Undara. Further along the highway are detours to Einasleigh Gorge, Forsayth and the delightful Cobbold Gorge. Boat tours through this stunning and extremely narrow gorge, flanked by thirty-metre-high cliffs, are not to be missed.

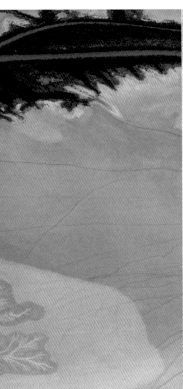

A farmer from Innot Hot Springs, Ravenshoe, takes a break **Photo:** Sara-Jane Cleland

WHERE
This 720-kilometre route runs from Cairns to the Gulf of Carpentaria, Queensland.

WHEN
During the Wet (December to April), roads in the Gulf savannah region may become impassable.

HOW
The Kennedy Highway is sealed, but be careful on the one-lane strips, and stay out of the way of road trains and other trucks. Forming a major section of Savannah Way, the Gulf Developmental Road is the main route into the Gulf from the east. It leaves the Kennedy Highway south of Mount Garnet, passing through Georgetown and Croydon en route to Normanton. The first section of the highway is in reasonably good condition, but after Georgetown the sealed surface narrows and deteriorates; this section is sometimes impassable during the Wet.

The gold-rush town of Croydon, about 150 kilometres east of Normanton, was established in 1885. Chinese and European gold miners rushed here so fast that the area had 8000 residents and twenty-six hotels just four years later. The historic *Gulflander* train runs weekly between Croydon and Normanton, which is close to the Gulf.

The beautiful Leichhardt Lagoon, just before Normanton, is a top spot for bird-watching. If you're lucky you'll see up to fifty different bird species in one day.

Normanton, the Gulf's major town, is known for its distinctive Victorian-era train station (home to the *Gulflander*), and is a great fishing base, with the Norman River still coughing up some booming barramundi. Karumba, northwest on the Gulf of Carpentaria, serves up some beautiful sunsets and great fishing. Karumba Point is the only stretch of beach in the central savannah that can be accessed by road.

All frocked up for Opera in the Outback at Undara **Photo:** Paul Dymond

The *Savannahlander* travels the five-and-a-half-hour journey between Mount Surprise, Einasleigh and Forsayth weekly, while the historic *Gulflander* does a weekly four-hour run from Croydon to Normanton.

Undara Experience (07-4097 1411) runs tours of the Undara lava tubes from Cairns. Cobbold Gorge Camping (07-4062 5470) takes visitors on electric boats that silently glide along the magical, narrow Cobbold Gorge. Oz Tours Safaris (07-4055 9535) has a seven-day Gulf Savannah tour, and Australian Pacific Tours (1800 675 222) runs tours from Cairns also.

Taking a dip at Indarri Falls, Boodjamulla (Lawn Hill) National Park **Photo:** Ross Barnett

Mining Country: Mount Isa Area

Aesthetically and geographically, Mount Isa is a long way from anywhere, but it's worth exploring this area along the Matilda Highway for a few days. Inland Queensland's major town, 'the Isa' revolves around its improbably rich copper, silver, lead and zinc mine, founded in 1924. Mount Isa's early days were pugilistic – the Isa Hotel built a 'bullring' for blokes to resolve their differences. These days the mine's massive 270-metre smelter punches through the skyline.

Also known as Kalkatungu, the local Kalkadoon people are one of the few tribes that can readily be named by white Australians. This stems from their fierce resistance to invasion, culminating in a desperate last stand in 1884. As pastoralism and mining pushed into their country during the 1860s, conflict inevitably arose. After 1878 the Kalkadoon waged guerrilla-style raids on pastoralists. In September 1884, 600 Kalkadoon occupied 'Battle Moun-

tain', twenty-two kilometres southwest of Kajabbi, where they fought their final battle against Native Police and armed settlers. Despite valiant resistance, their spears and clubs were no match for firearms and the Kalkadoon were cut down mercilessly. An estimated 900 Kalkadoon were killed between 1878 and 1884.

Mount Isa's Kalkadoon Tribal Culture Keeping Place preserves, promotes and increases public awareness of Kalkadoon culture, artefacts and spirituality with regular talks and tours to local rock-art sites. The Frank Aston Underground Museum, also in Mount Isa, houses the Kalkadoon Cultural Learning Centre, a display created by Mount Isa's indigenous people. Two walkways leading into Mount Isa's Underground Hospital have been planted with more than fifty plant species traditionally used by the Kalkadoon as bush medicine.

My dad was one of the best bull riders in the fifties and sixties. He actually lived at the Mount Isa rodeo ground, so it's running through my veins.

– Deb

Ochre painting of human figures at Sun Rock, near Mount Isa **Photo:** Ross Barnett

Smokestacks and Mt Isa city at dusk **Photo:** Ross Barnett

East of Mount Isa, Cloncurry features John Flynn Place – an ultra-modern museum telling the history of the Royal Flying Doctor Service (RFDS), founded here by Reverend John Flynn, a minister with the Australian Inland Mission (which he also helped establish). In 1928, the first RFDS flight winged its way from Cloncurry to Julia Creek, 134 kilometres to the east.

The Matilda Highway continues north from here. Riversleigh's monumental deposit of twenty-million-year-old fossils near Boodjamulla (Lawn Hill) National Park (p142), northwest of Mount Isa, is accessible from this route.

Karumba (p67) marks the end of the Matilda Highway at the Gulf of Carpentaria. Nearby, to the southeast, is Normanton, which boomed in the 1890s following the gold rush at Croydon (p67).

Dressed to break a bucking bronco, Mount Isa Rodeo **Photo:** Ross Barnett

WHERE
Mount Isa and the Matilda Highway are in far-western Queensland.

WHEN
Winter nights freeze, while summer temperatures nudge fifty degrees Celsius. Come for the mild days between April and October. In summer, the Wet floods the Gulf country.

The Mount Isa Show and the Normanton Rodeo & Gymkhana boot-scoot take place every June, while the Mount Isa Rotary Rodeo and the Normanton Ball and Races happen in August. Karumba sparkles with the Karumba Kapers (July), the Barra Ball (November) and the Fisherman's Ball (December).

HOW
The Mount Isa area is accessible by car along the fully sealed Matilda Highway. Major car-rental and coach companies have Mount Isa branches. Trains and planes arrive from Brisbane, Townsville and Cairns.

The Kalkadoon Tribal Culture Keeping Place (07-4749 1435) takes half-day tours with a Kalkadoon guide to three rock-art sites close to Mount Isa – Sun Rock, Porcupine Dreaming and Warrigal Dreaming.

The old Qantas hangar at Longreach Airport, the airline's original headquarters **Photo:** Ross Barnett

From Fossils to Flying Machines: Longreach Area

Longreach, resting on a 'long reach' of the Thomson River in Iningai country, is western Queensland's largest town after Mount Isa. After early explorations by colonialists in the 1850s, Longreach became a stock-route pit stop and was officially gazetted in 1887. The railway arrived in 1892, and the early twentieth-century wool boom brought serious money.

In February 1921, the first Qantas flight left here for Winton, 177 kilometres northwest of Longreach in Guwa country. Longreach became Qantas' headquarters, and the first seven Australian aircraft were cobbled together here between 1922 and 1930. The Qantas Founders' Outback Museum is at Longreach Airport.

Also in Longreach is the Stockman's Hall of Fame & Outback Heritage Centre. Pastoralism owed much of its

success to Aboriginal men and women, whose roles are acknowledged in a lamentably small corner of this otherwise fine museum.

Carisbrooke Station, southwest of Winton, sits amid the stark mesas of Cory's Range. The station runs tours to a rock-art site on the property, which includes hand stencils, ochre crosses, ceremonial bora rings and an initiation site.

Lark Quarry Conservation Park, south of Carisbrooke Station, features the fossilised footprints of a dinosaur dance party 100 million years ago.

South of Longreach are the Matilda Highway towns of Ilfracombe, Barcaldine, Blackall, Augathella, Charleville and Cunnamulla. Near Blackall is Blacks Palace, the most extensive rock-art site in Queensland's Central Highlands

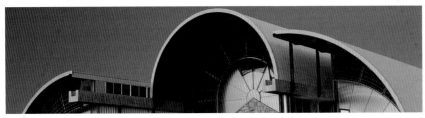

The curvaceous lines of the Australian Stockman's Hall of Fame at sundown **Photo:** Ross Barnett

and Australia's largest stencil-art site. Sandstone cliff overhangs house spectacular galleries with engravings, stencils, colourful freehand paintings and axe-grinding grooves. Parts of the site originally contained burial sites but have been badly vandalised. Aramac Station near Barcaldine contains an awesome 120-metre-long rock-art site, once a great meeting place, estimated to be 10,000 to 12,000 years old. There are thousands of pecked engravings of footprints, boomerangs, giant megafauna tracks and a twenty-metre-long serpent.

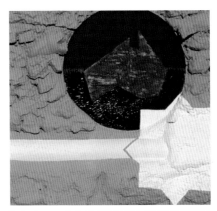

Design for a new Australian flag based on the Eureka Flag and incorporating the Aboriginal flag, Winton **Photo:** Ross Barnett

WHERE
This stretch of the Matilda Highway is in southwestern Queensland.

WHEN
Winter nights out here can be damn chilly, while summer days boil themselves dry. Time your visit with the temperate days between April and October.

Longreach, with nearby towns, hosts Easter in the Outback, the Outback Muster Drovers Reunion in May and the Diamond Shears Shearing Championships in July. Barcaldine's Artesian Festival (Mardi Gras and golf) gets swinging in June. In late August, Cunnamulla celebrates the World Lizard Racing Championships, a week-long arts, crafts and reptilian sports fest, and Winton's quirky Outback Festival is held every odd year in September.

HOW
The Longreach area is accessible by car along the fully sealed Matilda Highway and by train and plane from Brisbane, Townsville and Rockhampton.

The Longreach Outback Travel Centre (07-4658 1776) has a Longreach tour with dinner cruise on the Thomson River. There's also a merino station tour and outings to Barcaldine, Winton and Ilfracombe. Carisbrooke Station (07-4657 3984) is eighty-seven kilometres southwest of Winton. Outback Aussie Tours (1300 787 890) has package tours to Lark Quarry. Access to the Aramac Station site is through Artesian Country Tours (07-4651 2211).

71

Great balls of fire: straddling the Devil's Marbles **Photo:** Ross Barnett

Rainbow-Serpent Eggs:
Tennant Creek & the Devil's Marbles

For anyone travelling up the Stuart Highway from Alice Springs to Darwin (or back again), Tennant Creek is bound to be a stopover, because, along with Katherine, it's the only place around here that resembles a decent-sized town.

Known as Jurnkurakurr to the Warumungu people, Tennant Creek has grown up around a sacred site associated with a Spiky-Tailed Lizard Ancestor. The Dreaming stories of Jurnkurakurr – among them the snake, white cockatoo, budgerigar, fire and lightning – are depicted in a large mural on the wall of the Central Land Council office, in the centre of town. The town's more recent history is also in evidence and includes the restored telegraph buildings that formed part of the engineering wonder that was the Overland Telegraph, as well as daily tours of a historic gold-crushing plant and underground tunnel dating from the small gold rush here of the 1930s.

You can immerse yourself in indigenous culture at several centres in town, including the excellent Nyinkka Nyunyu Cultural Centre, with an arid zone ethno-botanical garden, two traditional dance rings (performance areas), and galleries and exhibition spaces. Ask here about visiting Julalikari Arts & Crafts in the Ngalpa Ngalpa community at the north end of town, where you can see Aboriginal women gather to paint traditional and contemporary art. At Anyinginyi Congress you can watch local craftspeople making boomerangs and other wooden objects.

But the highlight of the area is the bizarre rock formation 110 kilometres south of Tennant Creek, near Wauchope, known as the Devil's Marbles. Created by millennia of erosion, these huge round boulders appear to have been scattered on the landscape by a giant hand, balancing on one another in precarious fashion. Like Uluru (p88) they

Detail from a Jurnkurakurr Dreaming story painted on a wall of the Central Lands
Council office, Tennant Creek **Photo:** Ross Barnett

WHERE
Tennant Creek is in the
Northern Territory, 506
kilometres north of Alice
Springs, off the Stuart
Highway.

WHEN
June to October is the
best time to visit, and best
of all is late September,
when the eight-day Desert
Harmony Festival of Arts &
Culture is held, featuring
poetry readings and trad-
itional dance and rock-
band performances.

HOW
Tennant Creek, the Devil's
Marbles and the Pebbles
are all easily accessible
from the main road. South
of town, Kraut Downs
Station (08-8962 2820,
0417 828 959) runs
informative half-day tours
where you can learn about
bush tucker and medicine,
try whip-cracking and
boomerang-throwing and
enjoy billy tea and damper
(bush bread cooked over an
open fire). Devil's Marbles
Tours (0418 891 711)
offers trips to the Devil's
Marbles, including a bar-
becue lunch; the Tourist's
Rest Tennant Creek Hostel
(08-8962 2719) also runs
day trips to the Devil's
Marbles.

change colour with the light, and are surrounded by mysterious shadows and pale ghost gums. According to Aboriginal
mythology, the 'marbles' are eggs laid by the Rainbow Serpent. This striking area is rich in the Creation stories of the
Alyawarre, Anmatyerre, Kaytej and Warumungu people, and
caves under the rocks are the homes of ancestral beings.

Twelve kilometres north of Tennant Creek is the turn-off
west to the Pebbles (known as Kundjarra to Aboriginal
people), a formation of granite boulders that resemble a
miniaturised version of the better-known Devil's Marbles.
This is a women's sacred dancing site which people are
welcome to visit.

Red pillar box in Tennant Creek
Photo: Philip & Karen Smith

Driving the Outback

Outback driving can be heaps of fun but shouldn't be taken lightly – the last thing you want is to break down or get bogged in a remote area with no communications. There are plenty of routes open to conventional vehicles, but if you seriously want to explore you'll need a well-prepared four-wheel drive. Conditions vary widely and you need to be ready to handle them.

• Always carry plenty of water; a first aid kit; a good set of maps; a torch and spare batteries; and a compass. Also carry essential tools and spares, including at least two tyres, a tyre pressure gauge and an air pump.

• Load your vehicle evenly and keep heavier items in the vehicle itself and only light items on the roof rack. The lighter the load in general, the better your fuel economy and the less likely you are to have tyre wear or get bogged.

• Have your vehicle serviced and checked for mechanical condition before you leave, particularly the cooling system and the tyres. On the road, check the oil level each day, and tyre pressure every couple of days. It's a good idea to inflate your tyres a bit above the recommended maximum, especially if you're fully loaded.

• Distances between fill-ups can be long in the outback, so check locations and opening times of service stations and carry spare fuel and provisions.

• Check road conditions at the nearest tourist office, or see www.roadreport.nt.gov.au or other websites listed in this book.

• Heavy rain will quickly change conditions and turn roads into muddy skating rinks – many roads become impassable when wet and you will need to wait until the road has dried.

• Dirt roads are often bone-shakingly corrugated. The most comfortable and least dangerous way to deal with these is to keep an even speed. Similarly, don't speed on gibber plains, you'll inevitably end up changing your tyres. And remove your hubcaps if you don't want to lose them!

• Take care at creek crossings and take note of the water level markers or use a stick to gauge the water's depth before you proceed. Often it's not the water that is the problem but the steep banks on each side.

• Bulldust can be hazardous as the fine particles in the air can give the impression of a clear road ahead. Take care when overtaking and pull off the road if a passing vehicle creates excessive dust.

• If your vehicle is struggling through deep sand, deflating your tyres a bit will help.

• Collisions with wandering animals can be a real hazard. Kangaroos are most active around dawn and dusk. If you see one hopping across the road, slow right down – its friends are probably just behind it. If one hops out right in front of you, hit the brakes and only swerve to avoid the animal if it is safe to do so. If possible, avoid travelling at night on the highway.

• Watch out for road trains. These huge trucks can be as long as fifty metres, and you'll need a long distance and plenty of speed when overtaking. On single-lane roads you need to get right off the road if one approaches, because you can be sure it won't!

• There are still a lot of roads in central and northern Australia where the official recommendation is that you report to the police before you leave one end, and again when you arrive at the other. That way if you fail to turn up at the other end they can send a search party. At the very least, tell a friend or relative of your route and schedule.

• The Automobile Association of the Northern Territory (AANT; 8981 3837) provides an emergency breakdown service. Reciprocal arrangements exist with the state motoring organisations in Australia and similar organisations overseas.

• Mobile phones are often out of range and useless in the outback. An extra safety net is to hire a satellite phone, high frequency (HF) radio or EPIRB (Emergency Position Indicating Radio Beacon). For use only in emergencies, the EPIRB sends out a distress signal allowing rescuers to locate you. Another handy gadget to have is a GPS (global positioning system).

• Do not leave the main road. In an emergency, stay with your vehicle as it's easier to spot than you are. But don't sit inside it as it will become an oven. If you need to attract help, start a fire – a burning tyre creates a lot of smoke.

All aboard! The legendary *Ghan* chugs its way from Adelaide to Darwin, via the Alice Photo: Holger Leue

Camels & Caterpillar Beings: Alice Springs

Alice Springs, aka 'the Alice', is a robust, brawling desert town with a crop of heritage buildings, set amid the rugged red hills and ridges of the MacDonnell Ranges (p78). This is Arrernte country, the red centre of Australia, pretty much as far from the coast in any direction as you can get.

The Arrernte have five distinct dialect subgroups: Central, Northern, Southern, Eastern and Western. Alice Springs (Mparntwe) is the traditional country of the Central Arrernte, the smallest subgroup; about twenty per cent of the town's 27,000 folks are of Aboriginal descent. To the Central Arrernte, most of the landforms in and around the town were created by groups of Caterpillar Ancestors. One group (the Utnerrengetye) travelled from Mount Zeil to the west, while the others (the Ntyarlke and Yeperenye) came from Emily Gap (p80) to the east. The local Arrernte consider themselves direct descendants of these Caterpillar beings.

The lookout on top of Anzac Hill (Untyeyetweleye) has an awesome view of the town and MacDonnell Ranges. To the Arrernte, the hill is riddled with ancestry, including a Corkwood Woman whose spirit lives in the ground. Signs at the lookout give the totemic associations of thirteen cultural sites.

Just out of town, the Alice Springs Desert Park backs onto the red walls of Mount Gillen. You can learn about Aboriginal traditions from local guides and get acquainted with the unique biology of arid Australia. Southeast of town, Olive Pink Botanic Garden showcases native desert plants. The gardens honour Olive Pink, the original curator and great advocate for Aboriginal rights. You'll find the final resting place of the great Western Arrernte watercolourist, Albert Namatjira, in the Alice Springs Cemetery. The headstone – of red sandstone – features a terracotta-tile mural of three of Namatjira's ancestral Dreaming sites in the MacDonnell Ranges.

It's a long way between drinks **Photo:** Richard I'Anson

Alice Springs has a bit of a penchant for quirky festivals.
The Beanie Festival, held in July, is a hands-on event
featuring beanies (head-hugging hats designed for warmth).
You can watch Aboriginal women using traditional spin-
ning techniques to make yarn from just about anything:
unwashed sheep's wool, kangaroo fur, camel hair, human
hair, emu feathers, budgie feathers! Then they crochet the
beanies – emu-feather beanies are popular. Other activities
include demonstrations of basket-weaving using spinifex
(a spiky desert grass), and a fashion parade featuring
Aboriginal-made and batik fabrics. The Camel Cup, a series
of camel races, also takes place in July. But the event that
probably draws the biggest crowds of all takes place in
September: the Henley-on-Todd Regatta. The boats are all
bottomless, so the crews simply run up and down in the
(usually) dry riverbed.

The way we were: a mural on the wall of
Coles supermarket **Photo:** Wayne Walton

Shades of Namatjira: the late afternoon sun kisses Mount Sonder (Rwetyepme) in West MacDonnell National Park **Photo:** John Hay

Gaps & Gorges:
MacDonnell Ranges

Sweeping from east to west for over 400 kilometres, the timeless MacDonnell Ranges form a rugged red barrier across the vast central Australian plain. The ranges consist mainly of a parallel series of steep-sided ridges that rise up to 600 metres above the valley floors. Scattered through-out are deep gorges carved by ancient rivers that meander south into the vast Simpson Desert (p90).

The ranges are home to a huge variety of native plants, including many tall trees such as the majestic ghost gum. In hidden, moist places there are relics of the rainforest flora that covered this region millions of years ago. From Alice Springs (p76), the road through the MacDonnell Ranges is extremely scenic for the most part, taking you through a jumble of high ridges and hills drained by gum-lined creeks. Along the way are several parks and reserves where you can stop off to explore rugged gorges and Aboriginal culture.

The major attraction in the West MacDonnell Ranges is Simpsons Gap (Tyunpe to Central Arrernte people), a narrow gorge with towering red cliffs. The gap is linked to Perentie (large monitor lizard) and Eagle Ancestors of the Central Arrernte people; a cluster of jagged rocks high up on its eastern side marks the spot where two Perentie brothers took revenge on some devil men who had killed a number of their relatives. Interesting displays at the visitors centre and Simpsons Gap provide information on Tnengkare (the Western Arrernte Creation Time), rock engravings, ochre and the Creation stories of Tyunpe.

Another stunning feature is Standley Chasm (Angkerle). The chasm is famous for its midday light display of sun and shadow. The walk to the chasm is along a gully crammed with majestic river red gums, cycad palms and ferns.

Going for a spin at Glen Helen Gorge **Photo:** John Hay

Beautiful Serpentine Gorge is watched over by Wedge-Tailed Eagle and Water Serpent Ancestors of the Western Arrernte people. This is a traditional sanctuary area for wildlife and plants – hunting and gathering is strictly prohibited, as is swimming.

West of here are the Ochre Pits. Ochre *(ulpa)* was of great importance to the Western Arrernte. Except for a small deposit of yellow ochre, which is still used today, the material at this minor quarry site is of poor quality.

At Ormiston Gorge (Kwartetweme), the main water hole is a registered sacred site associated with an Emu Ancestor. The area around the water hole was once an important ceremonial ground. At the visitors centre, a dot painting and taped song, both by the site's traditional custodian, tells the story of the Emu's travels.

Fluffy pink mulla mulla amongst the long grasses in West MacDonnell National Park **Photo:** John Hay

WHERE
The MacDonnell Ranges stretch 161 kilometres west and 100 kilometres east of Alice Springs in the Northern Territory.

WHEN
April to September is the most pleasant time to visit this region.

HOW
Hiking enthusiasts will adore the Larapinta Trail, which runs for 223 kilometres along the spine of the West MacDonnell Ranges from Alice Springs to Mount Sonder; note that most sections are too remote and rugged for inexperienced walkers without a guide. If you like biking, don't miss the Simpsons Gap Bicycle Path, from Flynns Grave to Simpsons Gap (seventeen kilometres).

Spearing between high ridgelines, the road from Alice Springs through the West MacDonnells is sealed as far as the Finke River crossing near Glen Helen, 135 kilometres from town. West of here the road is normally rough dirt, with numerous wash-outs after heavy rain.

The Western Arrernte community of Wallace Rockhole (08-8956 7993), 115 kilometres southwest of Alice, runs a rock-art tour that includes a short bushwalk covering the traditional uses of many plants. Two Alice Springs–based companies include the rock-art tour in their itineraries: Alice Springs Holidays (08-8953 1411) does a three-day

(continued on p81)

79

Ghost gums against a red escarpment in Serpentine Gorge **Photo:** Richard l'Anson

The water hole at the entrance to Glen Helen Gorge (Yapulpa) was a major refuge in times of drought for the Western Arrernte. Yapulpa is linked to Itye, the Moon Man, who visited here while looking for a bride. Mount Sonder (Rwetyepme), to the northwest, is linked to several totemic beings, including a euro (a large wallaby species) from the Western Desert.

From the Tyler Pass lookout you get a nice view south to a prominent circular ridge, Gosse Bluff (Tnorala). This striking crater-like feature was formed during the Creation Time, when a group of Milky Way women danced across the sky. In order to dance, a mother put her baby down in its wooden baby-carrier, which then tumbled over the edge of the dancing area and crashed to earth, forming the rock walls of Tnorala.

Heading into the East MacDonnell Ranges, past the Stuart Highway, you arrive at Emily Gap (Anthwerrke to Central Ar-

rernte people), the first of two scenic gaps in Emily & Jesse Gaps Nature Park. A registered sacred site, this is one of the most important Creation sites in the Alice Springs area – it was from here that many of the Caterpillar ancestral beings of Mparntwe (Alice Springs) originated. Low down on the cliff-face inside the gorge there are some faded red-and-white paintings depicting the Caterpillar story.

Next you cross eroded flats with the Heavitree Range looming large on your left, and then enter a valley between red ridges. Corroboree Rock, one of a number of unusual, tan-coloured dolomite hills scattered over the valley floor, is known to Eastern Arrernte people as Antanangantana and is a registered sacred site. This unusual dog-toothed outcrop is associated with a Perentie Ancestor of the Eastern Arrernte. Despite the name, it is doubtful that the rock was ever used as a corroboree area, as there is no surface water in the vicinity. It is not clear why the site is of such significance to Aborigines, but sacred objects were stored here,

Rollercoasting over the MacDonnells **Photo:** John Hay

tour via Wallace Rockhole to Watarrka National Park (p84) and Uluru (p88); and
Sahara Adventures (1800 806 240) does a five-day camping tour to Uluru, Watarrka, Palm Valley and the West MacDonnell Ranges. Centremen Tours (08-8952 6708) visits Glen Helen Gorge and other attractions in the West MacDonnells on day tours from Alice Springs. Sahara Adventures (1800 806 240) includes Glen Helen Gorge on its five-day camping tour to Uluru, Watarrka, Wallace Rockhole and the West MacDonnells.

Most points of interest in the East MacDonnell Ranges are reached off the sealed Ross Highway, which links Alice Springs to the Ross River homestead. Further east, the unsealed roads can be quite rough. Access to N'Dhala Gorge is suitable for four-wheel drives only. Emu Run Tours (08-8953 7057) does day tours of the East McDonnells.

in a small cave in the rock, and it is thought that important ceremonial activities were also held here.

The N'Dhala Gorge Nature Park is another important religious site. This deep, rugged gorge known as Irlwentye contains thousands of rock engravings, as well as several painting sites and rock shelters. The engravings, most of which date from within the past 2000 years, are of two styles: pounded and finely pecked. Designs include concentric circles, animal tracks and human figures. You'll see a number of engravings along the one-kilometre walking track that leads into the main gorge.

Enjoying a playful dip in the waterhole at Emily Gap (Anthwerrke) **Photo:** Ross Barnett

The Red Cabbage Palms that thrive in Palm Valley are not found anywhere else in the world **Photo:** John Banagan

Palm Trees & Water Holes: Finke Gorge

A few hours west of Alice Springs (p76), the 46,000-hectare Finke Gorge National Park is one of central Australia's premier wilderness areas, featuring high red cliffs, stately river red gums, cool water holes, clean white sand and clumps of tall palms. From the Hermannsburg Mission north of the park, four-wheel-drive tracks head south to Palm Valley and Boggy Hole. Both routes run through the meandering Finke Gorge.

For thousands of years the Finke River formed part of an Aboriginal trade route that brought red ochre from the south and pearlshell from the north. The area was a drought refuge for the Western Arrernte people, who drank from soaks in the sandy riverbed.

Shaded by tall river red gums and date palms, the whitewashed Hermannsburg Mission was founded in 1876.

Despite incredible hardships and white-settler opposition to their protection of Aborigines from genocide, the Lutheran missionaries established central Australia's first township. Hermannsburg's population once included 700 Western Arrernte people. In 1982, title was handed back to the Arrernte. Most of them have since left to establish thirty-five small outstation communities on traditional clan territories.

Palm Valley (Mpulungkinya), the national park's main attraction, is steeped in Western Arrernte culture and is home to over 300 plant species. The palms and cycads in this lush oasis represent young Fire Ancestors who, having been burned in a huge bushfire to the north, were picked up by strong winds and dropped in Mpulungkinya. Shaggy palm fronds represent their traditional headdresses, dark trunks their fire-blackened bodies.

The whitewashed Hermannsburg church **Photo:** John Banagan

A haven for water birds and fish, Boggy Hole is one of only a handful of permanent water holes in the Finke system. In the 1880s there was a police camp here from which Mounted Constable William Willshire and his Aboriginal troopers quelled black resistance to white settlement with indiscriminate slaughter. The Hermannsburg missionaries protested so vigorously that the police were moved in 1893 and Willshire brought to trial for his excesses. He wasn't convicted, but his bloody career was ended.

A red monolith overlooks the Amphitheatre, Palm Valley
Photo: John Banagan

WHERE
Finke Gorge is in the Northern Territory, 122 kilometres west of Alice Springs.

WHEN
Central Australian summers are stinkers, so come in the cooler winter months (June to August). If you must travel in summer, carry a high-frequency radio, plenty of drinking water and drive with another vehicle. Finke Gorge is no place to be when heavy rain sets in, which happens about once a year, usually in summer.

HOW
For information on Finke Gorge conditions and walking tracks, call the Parks and Wildlife Service (08-8951 8250) in Alice Springs, or the Palm Valley ranger (08-8956 7401). Four-wheel drives need a minimum fuel range of 650 kilometres to tackle the area. For the Boggy Hole Track, you'll need a four-wheel drive with low-range gearing and good ground clearance. The track crosses Aboriginal land; you don't need a permit to use the road, but you must stick to the main route. Camping is prohibited. The Hermannsburg Mission doesn't require a permit, but residential areas are off-limits.

Day tours from Alice Springs to Hermannsburg and Palm Valley are run by AAT Kings Tours (08-8952 1700), NT Luxury Day Tours (08-8952 7751), Palm Valley Day Tours (08-8952 0022) and the Alice Wanderer (08-8952 2111). Sahara Adventures (1800 806 240) visits Palm Valley, Hermannsburg and Wallace Rockhole (p79).

The red rock walls of Kings Canyon up close **Photo:** Krzysztof Dydynski

Native Cat Men: Kings Canyon

The 100-metre-high sheer cliffs of Kings Canyon and the complex microclimates within its sheltering walls make a visit to Watarrka (Kings Canyon) National Park mandatory if you're in the Uluru–Alice Springs area. More than 600 plant species have been recorded here – the highest plant diversity anywhere in Australia's deserts. The one-kilometre canyon has been carved from a towering sandstone plateau that's dotted with bizarre, weathered sandstone domes. At the head of the canyon are the cool, tranquil spring-fed pools of the Garden of Eden, a narrow gorge leading to a lush oasis of ferns and prehistoric cycads, and containing ripple rock and fossilised jellyfish. The deep waters here are surprisingly cold. The narrow, rocky bed of Kings Creek is punctured with tall ghost gums and unusual bonsai-like trees.

White explorer Ernest Giles travelled through this area in 1872 and found numerous Aboriginal people living here,

but by the 1920s the country had been abandoned due to conflicts with pastoralists and loss of resources. Today, much of this land has been handed back to the Luritja people, traditional owners for at least 20,000 years. Watarrka is the Luritja name for the path taken by a large group of Kuningka (Native Cat Men) during Creation Time (Tjukurpa). These ancestors travelled up Kings Creek to the Kings Canyon Waterhole, where they held ceremonies before continuing their journey north.

The best way to appreciate Kings Canyon is to walk. The six-kilometre Kings Canyon Walk will make you puff around the canyon rim, offering views from the exposed ridge down to the water hole where the Kuningka danced. The route winds through the large, beehive-like sandstone domes that represent the bodies of young Kuningka. The Kathleen Springs Walk passes a deep pool inhabited by a giant Water

Ancient weathered cliffs at Kings Canyon Photo: Wayne Walton

Serpent. This permanent water hole was important to the nomadic Luritja and harboured abundant food plants, such as the native fig and plum bush. Contact the rangers for maps and information. If you have more time, the lovely two-day Giles Track, partly in the footsteps of Ernest Giles, links Kings Canyon with Kathleen Springs. There's plenty of wildlife to be seen, particularly around the water holes.

Teetering on the edge at Kings Canyon
Photo: Simon Richmond

WHERE
The Kings Canyon area is 400 kilometres southwest of Alice Springs, in the Northern Territory. Turn onto the Lasseter Highway from the Stuart Highway turn-off at Erldunda. After 110 kilometres turn right onto Luritja Road – it's 135 kilometres to Watarrka National Park.

WHEN
The summer heat is hard to take out here, but with sealed roads and Alice Springs and Yulara nearby, it's easy to visit any time of year.

HOW
Many Alice Springs operators offer tours to Kings Canyon. Contact Central Australian Tourism (08-8952 5800) for details. If you're taking your own vehicle out of Alice, drive via Erldunda to stay on the sealed surface. Taking the dirt Ernest Giles Road will save you about 150 kilometres, but a more scenic option is to head west from Alice via Larapinta Drive to the unsealed Mereenie Loop Road. Several bus companies run services between Kings Canyon and Alice Springs or Yulara.

You'll need a permit to travel to Watarrka along the Mereenie Loop Road, which passes through Aboriginal land. Permits are issued in Alice Springs by the Central Land Council (08-8951 6320) and Central Australian Tourism, as well as the Hermannsburg service station and the Kings Canyon and Glen Helen Resorts. You can contact the rangers on 08-8956 7488.

The standout cliffs of Rainbow Valley **Photo:** John Banagan

Rainbow Rocks:
South of Alice Springs

The country south of Alice is varied, with much of it dominated by the red sand dunes of the western Simpson Desert
(p90). In early spring, after good rains, the whole area is
ablaze with wildflowers.

The Ewaninga Conservation Reserve, thirty-nine kilometres
out of Alice on the rough and dusty Old South Road, protects Aboriginal rock peckings carved into a small outcrop
of sandstone rocks. Senior Eastern Arrernte custodians of
the site say that the meaning of the symbols is sacred and
too dangerous to reveal to the uninitiated.

Southeast of Alice Springs is the Eastern Arrernte community of Santa Teresa (Ltyentye Apurte), built on a sacred
rainmaking site. Keringke Arts – an association of local
women artists – is known for its unique contemporary designs and vibrantly colourful style. The art centre normally

displays a range of high-quality work; to see it you need to
call to arrange a visitor's permit.

The Mac Clark Conservation Reserve protects a large stand
of tall waddy (Acacia peuce) trees. This rare and unusual
species is found in only three places in the world: near
Boulia and Birdsville in Queensland, and here. The waddy
grows very slowly to a height of up to seventeen metres and
can live for 500 years. Named after the Aboriginal fighting
clubs that are said to have been made from its wood, the
species owes its survival to its long, needle-like foliage,
which has only a small surface exposed to the sun and wind
and so suffers little moisture loss.

At Chambers Pillar Historical Reserve, 160 kilometres south
of Alice Springs, the main attraction is Itirkawara, a red-and-
yellow sandstone column that rises fifty metres above the

WHERE
This Northern Territory route loops down from Alice to Finke (Aputula; about 240 kilometres south) and back again.

WHEN
The entire Alice Springs to Finke (Aputula) route is closed over the Queen's Birthday weekend in June each year to allow the running of the Finke Desert Race.

HOW
You combine the two main tracks – the Old Andado Track and Finke Track – as a loop from Alice Springs. The Old Andado Track can usually be negotiated with care by conventional vehicles with good ground clearance. A permit is not required to transit straight through Santa Teresa, but visits to the community must be arranged in advance. NT Luxury Day Tours (08-8952 7751) and the Outback Experience (08-8953 2666) both visit Rainbow Valley and Itirkawara.

sand plain. This striking feature is an important Dreaming site for the Southern Arrernte people, and was a landmark for early nonindigenous travellers. Itirkawara was a Knob-Tailed Gecko Ancestor of great strength and violent temper. In one incident he killed a number of other ancestors with his stone knife, then flouted the law by taking a girl of the wrong skin group to be his bride. The pair were banished to the desert where both turned to stone – Itirkawara became the Pillar and the girl Castle Rock, about 500 metres away.

The small Oak Valley Aboriginal community is between the old and new *Ghan* railway crossings on the Hugh River Stock Route. Nearby is the Rainbow Valley Conservation Reserve, best visited in the early morning or late afternoon (especially in winter), when the sandstone cliffs' rainbow-coloured bands are at their vibrant best. The reserve has several sites of significance to Southern Arrernte people – a large rock behind Rainbow Valley, at the western end of the reserve, is a registered sacred site. In the rocky hills to the southeast are several art sites, rock shelters and old camp sites that you may stumble across while you're bushwalking in the area. Most of the time the area around the reserve looks harsh and lifeless, but when the claypans are full of water it is one of central Australia's more extraordinary sights. In former times, after good rains filled the nearby claypan, this was an important place for hunting and gathering. It gave the people a chance to 'rest' the country around the longer-lasting water holes, and they would stay here until the claypan dried up again.

Below, from top: Sturt's desert pea sometimes pops up after the rains Photo: Martin Cohen; Itirkawara (Chambers Pillar), an ancestral being turned to stone Photo: David Curl

It's good medicine up here.
Good for the soul. – Deb

Storm clouds gather over Uluru (Ayers Rock), illuminated by the ruddy glow of sunset Photo: Chris Mellor

Many Moods, Many Heads:
Uluru & Kata Tjuta

The first sight of Uluru (Ayers Rock), towering above the surrounding pancake-flat plains like a lone iceberg in a rust-red ocean, will startle even the most jaded traveller. No matter how many times you've seen it in postcards, nothing quite prepares you for the real thing, with its intricate grooves, pockmarks, shadows and sheer size. The 'many moods of Uluru' are endlessly documented, but it's undeniably amazing to watch its dawn and dusk colour shifts. The other main feature of the World Heritage–listed Uluru-Kata Tjuta National Park is the bulbous, oddly intimate rock formations of nearby Kata Tjuta (literally 'Many Heads', also known as the Olgas).

Uluru is made up of a type of coarse-grained sandstone known as arkose, which was formed from sediment from eroded granite mountains. Kata Tjuta, on the other hand, is a conglomerate of granite and basalt gravel glued together by

mud and sand. The sedimentary beds that make up the two formations were laid down over a period of about 600 million years, in a shallow sea known to geologists as the Amadeus Basin. Various periods of uplift caused the beds to be buckled, folded and lifted above sea level, and those which form Uluru were turned so that they are almost vertical. For the last 300 million years or so erosion has worn away the surface rocks, leaving what we see today. Yet it's believed that Uluru extends up to five kilometres beneath the sand.

This area is of deep cultural significance to the local Pitjantjatjara and Yankunytjatjara people, who refer to themselves as Anangu. Archaeologists say Aboriginal people have inhabited this area for 22,000 years, but the Anangu believe they've been here since Creation Time (Tjukurpa), when the landscape was carved by ancestral beings: Kuniya (the Woman Python), Kurpany (an evil dog-like creature),

Rippling clouds fan across a Red Centre sundown Photo: Chris Mellor

WHERE
Uluru-Kata Tjuta National Park is in the Northern Territory, 400 kilometres southwest of Alice Springs. Yulara is 247 kilometres along the Lasseter Highway from the Stuart Highway turn-off at Erldunda; Uluru is a further eighteen kilometres. The Kata Tjuta turn-off is eight kilometres past Yulara, the rocks themselves forty-five kilometres further on.

WHEN
Yulara, the service village for Uluru-Kata Tjuta National Park, has effectively turned one of the world's least hospitable regions into an easy and comfortable place to visit any time of year.

HOW
The park entry station on the Yulara–Uluru road is open daily. You're better off travelling here independently, as organised tours tend to be regrettably brief. If you're not driving, several bus companies visit Uluru from Alice Springs; ask at the Central Australian Tourism office (08-8952 5800).

A slew of indigenous-run and other organised tours operate out of the Uluru Cultural Centre (08-8956 2299) and the Tour and Information Centre (08-8957 7324) at Yulara shopping centre. Various outfits offer sunrise, sunset, night sky, camel, motorbike, plane or helicopter tours.

Liru (the Brown Snake), Lungkarta (the Blue-Tongued Lizard) and Mala (the Rufous Hare Wallaby). The Anangu consider themselves direct descendants of these beings. They officially own the national park and have leased it to Parks Australia until 2084.

For years, climbing Uluru has been a visitor's rite of passage. For the Anangu, however, the path up the side of the rock is the route the ancestral Mala men took when they arrived here, and has considerable spiritual significance. Apart from that, as custodians of this land, the Anangu take responsibility for the safety of visitors. For these reasons, the Anangu don't climb Uluru, and request that you don't either.

Instead, there are plenty of established walks and viewing areas around Uluru and Kata Tjuta. The loop around the base is 9.4 kilometres.

Walpa Gorge at Kata Tjuta (The Olgas)
Photo: Richard l'Anson

Footprints on the crest of the Nappanerica Sand Dune (Big Red) **Photo:** John Hay

Dunes, Springs & Soaks: Simpson Desert

Recognised as one of the world's most outstanding examples of a sand-ridge desert, the Simpson sprawls across more than 150,000 square kilometres at the junction of the Northern Territory, Queensland and South Australian borders. The desert's most obvious characteristic is its remarkable system of parallel dunes, which rise to forty metres and stretch without a break for up to 200 kilometres. The desert has a number of major habitat types, including spinifex grasslands, gidgee (small acacia) woodlands and coolabah flood-outs. Collectively these are home to 800 plant species and over 300 animal species.

Spread over an area of about seventy square kilometres, Dalhousie Springs are the only natural source of permanent surface water in the area. The springs are so isolated from other permanent surface waters that they contain many species of aquatic fauna found nowhere else. The main spring

is a steaming oasis of deep water measuring about 150 metres by fifty metres and fringed by low paperbark trees and reeds. A fantastic sight in its desolate setting, the pool attracts a large variety of wildlife, including goannas, water birds and dingoes. A swim in the hot pool is great on a cold winter's morning.

Approdinna Attora Knolls, two low flat-topped hills of white gypseous rock just south of the Northern Territory border, are an important landmark in this world of sand ridges and saltpans. They also offer some of the best views in the Simpson Desert. To the south of the knolls lies Wolporican Soak, one of the rare permanent sources of fresh water that allowed the desert's original inhabitants to survive here. In 1886 explorer David Lindsay found this soak, which was accessed by a well about four metres deep; on being cleaned out, it yielded forty litres in an hour. Wolporican

WHERE
The Simpson Desert covers 150,000 square kilometres, stretching into Queensland, the Northern Territory and South Australia.

WHEN
Travel is not recommended from October to April, when temperatures exceed forty degrees Celsius.

HOW
Rig Road takes you across the desert from Mount Dare homestead to Birdsville Track. It's the easiest route, though a four-wheel drive is needed. French Line and QAA Line (two access roads) cut across at right angles and should not be attempted by inexperienced desert drivers.

You'll need a day/night permit to visit Dalhousie Springs overnight. Passes can be bought at Department for Environment and Heritage (DEH; 08-8204 1910) or National Parks offices. Wider travel in the Simpson Desert within South Australia requires a Desert Parks Pass (1800 816 078). Camping permits are required if you want to spend a night.

Aboriginal Desert Discovery Tours (www.backpackerto urs.com.au/Tour_compan ies/NT/alice_springs/Abori gina_Cultural_Discovery _Tours.htm), an Aboriginal-owned enterprise of Pwerte Marnte Marnte Aboriginal Corporation & Austours, runs tours to the Simpson Desert. Diamantina Touring Company (03-5777 0681) and Outback Tag-a-Long Tours (02-6025 6494) run four-wheel-drive tours.

was a major habitation site for the Wangkangurru people, who inhabited the desert's central and southern sections prior to 1900. Searching around the edge of claypans throughout the Simpson will often reveal evidence of Aboriginal occupation in the form of stone tools and grinding stones, all of which were carried in from far away. (Note that the collection of such artefacts is illegal and hefty fines can result if you're caught with any in your possession.)

As you approach Birdsville (p94) the Simpson Desert's last gasp rises in front of you as a towering wall of pale red sand: the Nappanerica Sand Dune. More commonly known as Big Red, this forty metre-high monster is said to be the desert's highest sand dune.

Above left: Artichokes cooking over a campfire dug into the sand
Photo: John Hay
Above centre: The scorching sun beats down on a Simpson dune
Photo: Jason Edwards
Above right: Sign of life: an animal burrow in the desert sand
Photo: Tony Wheeler

Responsible Travel

Responsible travel is about having respect for the local environment and culture, and looking out for your own safety. In the Australian bush you may find yourself in unfamiliar situations, and it's worth taking a moment to think before you act.

Some indigenous sites are registered under heritage legislation and have conditions attached, or may be visited only with permission from their traditional custodians or in their company. The wear and tear caused by large numbers of visitors, particularly in fragile ecosystems, places enormous pressure on these sites. Do resist the temptation to touch artworks, as the skin's natural oils can cause considerable deterioration. Dust also causes problems – move thoughtfully at rock-art sites and leave your vehicle some distance away. Please respect the wishes of indigenous custodians by reading signs carefully, keeping to dedicated camping areas and staying on marked tracks and boardwalks. Remember that indigenous rock art and engravings are manifestations of sacred beliefs and indigenous laws.

When interacting with indigenous Australians, you will generally find them very polite and willing to share their life and culture with you – but it must necessarily be on their terms. You should act with respect for privacy, and remember that your time constraints, sense of urgency and priorities may not always be shared. In some parts of Australia, English is not a first language, but in others many people speak English fluently. Body language and etiquette vary across the country: the terms 'thank you', or 'hello' and 'goodbye', may not be used in some areas, or direct eye contact may be avoided. So take note of local practices – take it as it comes and follow the cues. Be aware that some Aboriginal communities are 'dry', that is, there may be rules relating to the purchase and consumption of alcohol, or they may forbid any alcohol in the area at all.

Aboriginal crafts and artworks make great souvenirs and gifts. By buying authentic items you are supporting indigenous culture and helping to ensure that traditional and contemporary expertise and designs continue to be of economic and cultural benefit for individuals and communities. Unfortunately, much of the so-called indigenous art sold as souvenirs is fake, usually made overseas by underpaid workers. You can look for the swing tag on merchandise to determine its authenticity and support indigenous people. Artworks should have a certificate of authenticity. Note that haggling over price is not part of Aboriginal culture.

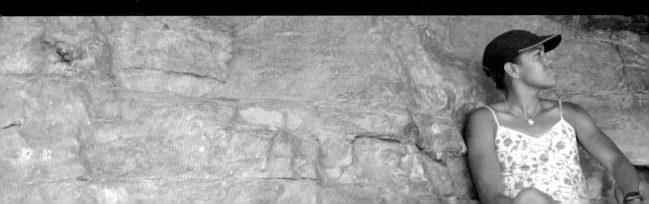

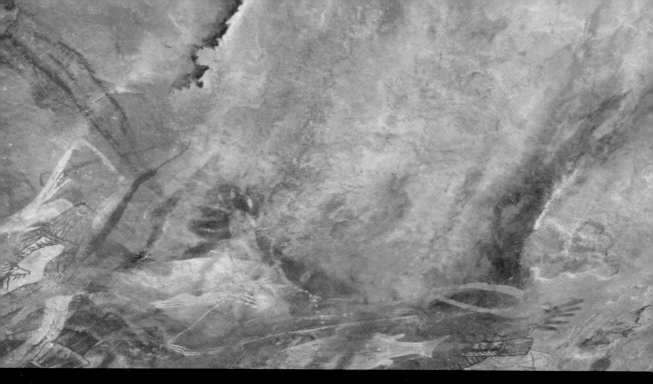

There are a range of protocols for visiting indigenous lands, but it is always courteous to make contact prior to your visit. In many cases you must acquire a permit to enter. Permits give Aboriginal landowners some administrative control over their land and recognise their rights to manage it. Check with local indigenous land councils and police stations before visiting to ensure that you do not break any rules and apply for permits as required. If you're travelling on organised tours, the tour operators will have made permit arrangements for you.

It's also important to respect the properties and livelihoods of the pastoralists whose land you will be passing through. Ask permission before pitching a tent, be sparing with water supplies, always leave gates as you find them, and keep your dog on a leash at all times when in sheep and cattle country.

To help preserve the ecology and beauty of the bush, carry all noncombustible rubbish in a heavy-duty plastic bag until you can dispose of it at an authorised dumping place (don't bury it, as animals will dig it up). Don't use detergents or toothpaste in or near watercourses, and if there are no available toilets, bury your waste away from watercourses to avoid contamination. Avoid trampling or removing the plant life, don't depend on open fires for cooking, and do not feed the wildlife as this can lead to animals becoming dependent on hand-outs, to unbalanced populations and to diseases. In national parks camping is usually only permitted in designated areas.

There are some simple safety precautions when travelling in the bush. When walking, be prepared for heat and always carry plenty of water (at least one litre per person per hour), and tell someone where you're going. Stick to marked trails or make sure you have a good map and compass and know how to use them. Among Australia's unique and lovable wildlife there are a few less cuddly bush inhabitants, although it's unlikely that you'll come face to face with many of them. Saltwater crocodiles are found in river estuaries and large rivers in the Top End, and you just can't get friendly with them, so before diving into that cool, inviting water take note of the warning signs. Australia has many species of snakes, and although few are dangerous or aggressive, the most venomous ones are very dangerous, so your best bet is to leave them all alone. Another serious hazard is animals – particularly kangaroos but also livestock – straying onto the road. The worst time to travel is between dusk and dawn.

A welcome cold drink at the Mungeranie Hotel **Photo:** John Hay

Skeletons & Gibbers:
Birdsville Track

Seared by the relentless sun and scoured by countless raging dust storms, the Birdsville Track gained notoriety as one of Australia's most hazardous stock routes. Linking a series of unreliable water holes and artesian bores across the continent's driest region, it was originally a droving highway along which up to 50,000 head of cattle a year walked from Queensland to the railway at Marree (p98) in South Australia. Apart from cattle, the track's main users until the 1930s were camel trains, in the care of Afghan cameleers, carrying supplies to and from Marree. Until relatively recent times it was little more than an ill-defined pad (animal track), with the bones of dead stock pointing the way to the next drink.

With a population of around 120, the town of Birdsville is set on a barren, stony rise overlooking the Diamantina River. Birdsville is best known for its tremendous heat waves (temperatures of fifty degrees Celsius are common in summer),

its annual race meeting and, of course, its association with the famous Birdsville Track. Aside from the Birdsville Working Museum, which houses a large and varied collection of memorabilia and machinery, there is little to see in town. A stand of rare waddy trees (p86), fourteen kilometres north, and a coolabah tree carved by Burke and Wills, two and a half kilometres south, are nearby attractions.

About a hundred kilometres south of Birdsville, the track leaves the floodplain and enters the armour-plated desolation of Sturts Stony Desert, an enormous wasteland of polished stones that explorer Charles Sturt crossed in 1845 on his search for the inland sea.

Further down the track is picturesque Mungeranie Gap. If you're here in the early morning or late afternoon, it's worth going for a walk among these colourful low hills to capture

WHERE
The 517-kilometre Birds-
ville Track links Birdsville
(Queensland) and Marree
(South Australia).

WHEN
Due to extreme summer
heat, April to October is
the best time to travel
the track. The famous
Birdsville Races, which
take place on the first
weekend in September,
see the population swell to
7000 or more as visitors
from all over Australia fly in
for the fun. Bushfly plagues
are the track's downside in
warm weather.

HOW
The track is a good dirt
road, but it is isolated
so it's essential to carry
ample drinking water at all
times (note that much of
the water along the way is
undrinkable).

Big Country Outback
Safaris (08-8538 7105)
travels from Adelaide along
the track to the Birdsville
Races. Cattle Drive Tours
(1300 366 770) gives you
the opportunity to participate in a cattle drive along
the track.

their stark beauty on film. The country changes to patchy
bare gibbers (stony areas) and low sand ridges on its way to
the Mungeranie Hotel, where a cold beer or two does wonders for dust-caked throats. The hotel is a stone's throw from
the Derwent River, where an oasis of shady trees is watered
by a flowing bore. Like other wetland areas on the track, this
is a fine spot for bird-watching. Half-dead coolabahs on the
nearby sand hill are roosting places for screeching flocks of
corellas, and water birds such as ducks, herons and native
hens are also common here.

Beyond Mulka, you say goodbye to the gibbers of Sturts
Stony Desert and enter a world of high yellow-sand ridges
that roll away on either side like jumbled waves on an
ocean. Known as the Natterannie Sandhills, this area marks
the convergence of the Strzelecki Desert to the east and
the Tirari Desert to the west. Parts of the Tirari, which runs
on to the eastern shore of Lake Eyre, are the closest thing
Australia has to true desert.

Above left: You don't want to take a
wrong turn out here
Above centre: A nostalgic sign at the
Birdsville Museum
Above right: The famous Birdsville Pub,
on the edge of the Simpson Desert
Photos: John Hay

Cath and I have no idea where we're going. We're
It will be about going into places and meeting people
lead us to another thousand adventures. —Deb

Vanishing point: the Strzelecki Track stretches towards infinity **Photo:** Peter Ptschelinzew

Ochre & Engravings: Strzelecki Track

What does a Polish-born, sometimes eccentric explorer who called himself a 'count' have to do with inland Australia? Not much really, since he never set foot in this region, but his name is immortalised in the track that bears his name. The Strzelecki Track runs through the arid expanse of north-eastern South Australia, between the northern extremity of the Flinders Ranges (p218) and Cooper Creek. Originally a stock route pioneered by a bushman who also happened to be a cattle thief, the track was largely unused before the discovery of gas and oil in the Cooper Creek basin in the early 1960s.

At the southern end of the route, north of the tiny hamlet of Lyndhurst (on the northern edge of the Flinders Ranges) and close to the Marree road, is an ochre quarry that was once worked by Aboriginal people. The ochre from this area was traded as far north as the Gulf of Carpentaria and south to the coast. Unlike many others, this quarry has never been mined by Europeans.

Cooper Creek has always been an important meeting place for Ngamini, Yawarawarka and Dieri people, particularly because of the area's permanent source of fresh water. When in flood, the waters of Cooper Creek feed Strzelecki Creek, which Charles Sturt stumbled upon in his search for an inland sea. An admirer of the geologist Paul Edmund de Strzelecki, who had discovered Mount Kosciuszko (Australia's highest mountain), Sturt named the creek after him (hence the name of the track). Not far from Innamincka spectacular rock engravings testify to the rich culture of the people who were once here. The rock engravings are at the far end of Cullyamurra Waterhole, close to the bottleneck on the Cooper known as the Innamincka Choke. If you are camped by the water hole, reputedly the deepest in central

readed North and that's pretty much it ... ed through meeting these people will

WHERE
The Strzelecki Track runs through South Australia from Lyndhurst, 560 kilometres north of Adelaide, to Innamincka, on historic Cooper Creek – a total distance of 483 kilometres.

WHEN
A picnic race meeting held in Innamincka each year, generally towards the end of August, really makes the place bounce. Accommodation is stretched at these times and even camping close to town can be crowded.

HOW
The Strzelecki Track is well defined, graded and normally passable to conventional vehicles. However, you need to be self-sufficient, as summer can be very hot, you will meet few other travellers and a breakdown can be life-threatening.

Australia at twenty-eight metres, you can get to the site by canoe. On sand hills all along the Cooper flood plain are old camp sites littered with stone chips and tools, and the evidence of past feasts (note that the collection of such artefacts is illegal).

European history is also in evidence at Cooper Creek, the site of the famous Dig Tree. The name relates to the message carved into the trunk of this coolabah by the men who eventually gave up waiting for the explorers Burke and Wills to return from their expedition to the interior: 'DIG 3FT N.W. APR. 21 1861.' By a cruel twist of fate the exhausted explorers returned just hours after the men left and, as the buried supplies weren't enough to revive them, they died on the banks of the creek. Sitting here under the shady trees watching a muddy river flow past, you cannot help but be struck by the irony of it all. The creek and its environs supported many hundreds of Aborigines and yet Burke and Wills starved to death.

When full, Coongie Lakes, 106 kilometres northwest of Innamincka, are a spectacular wetland alive with birds. The lakes, which form one of the arid outback's greatest freshwater lake systems, rely on the occasional flooding of the Cooper to fill them. Coongie Lake is the southernmost in this complex, and the only one you can visit.

Above, from top: Corellas congregating at Innamincka **Photo:** Russell Mountford; The Dig Tree, Cooper Creek, where the journey of Burke and Wills came to an end **Photo:** John Hay

Local tours can be arranged at the hotel or general store in Innamincka. Given enough warning, the tour guides can take you out to Coongie Lakes or along the Cooper to the Dig Tree and other historic places scattered along the waterway. The canoe trips of Cooper Creek and Coongie Lakes nearby, offered by Ecotrek (08-8383 7198), go past numerous indigenous sites. Depending on numbers, Cooper Discovery Tours (08-8675 9599) runs a two-hour return cruise from the Innamincka town common to King's Marker (a memorial at the spot where John King, the sole survivor of the Burke and Wills expedition, was found).

The Pink Roadhouse and its forecourt of dirt, Oodnadatta **Photo:** John Hay

Mound Springs: Oodnadatta Track

Besides having a great-sounding name (reportedly from *utnadata,* meaning 'mulga blossom'), the Oodnadatta Track is one of Australia's most interesting outback routes. As you cross the generally flat terrain of desert sand ridges and gibber plains (stony desert), the sense of space is profound. Its many attractions include artesian mound springs, Lake Eyre and numerous relics of the Overland Telegraph Line and Great Northern Railway.

This region is Australia's driest and the mound springs are its major natural source of fresh water. For Aborigines, explorers and settlers they served as stepping stones into the interior. Before the advent of white settlement, the local Aboriginal people used them as part of a major trade route that linked the Kimberley and Cape York to the southern coast via central Australia. This was the original Oodnadatta Track.

In Marree, at the southeastern end of the track, the Arabunna Centre has a haphazard museum with artefacts and early photographs of Arabunna people, and some carvings for sale. About seventy kilometres northwest of Marree is the Marree Man, a four-kilometre-long outline of an Aboriginal warrior and possibly the largest work of art in the world. Its origin is unknown (some say it was put there by personnel from one of the US bases), but it appeared in the desert sands in 1998. It can only be seen from the air.

Leaving Marree, the track passes through a rather ordinary-looking fence that is in fact the famous Dog Fence, built to keep dingoes from the sheep flocks grazing to its south, and the world's longest man-made barrier. Lake Eyre, the next major attraction on the route, covers a total area of 9700 square kilometres. When flooded (which happens every eight years on average), the lake becomes a vast breeding

OODNADATTA

ground for swarms of pelicans, seagulls, terns and many other water birds. Most times, however, the lake is little more than a blinding expanse of white salt crust.

Blanches Cup, at the foot of Wabma Kadarbu Mound Springs Conservation Park, is considered a classic mound spring due to the symmetry of its mound and the large circular pool on top. Mound springs, from which groundwater flows to the surface, are the natural outlets of the Great Artesian Basin, a vast sandstone aquifer formed some 100 to 250 million years ago and one of the world's largest artesian groundwater basins; its oldest waters date back almost two million years. The basin's water-bearing rocks in the eastern ranges of Queensland and New South Wales soak up rainfall, and from here the water moves towards South Australia, flowing at a rate of up to five metres per year. Like other springs, Blanches Cup has suffered greatly from introduced grazing animals and reduced flow rates, the latter due to many bores having been drilled into the aquifer. Nevertheless, the reed-fringed water hole remains a beautiful paradox among sun-baked salt flats.

Oodnadatta's heyday lasted from 1889 to 1927, when the town was the terminus for the Great Northern Railway. From here, camel trains made trips of up to 3000 kilometres to resupply distant communities. Today, half the town, including its hotel and general store, is owned by a council made up of Aborigines, who comprise the bulk of the population of about 200.

Above, from top: Planehenge, not far from Marree, is inspired by Stonehenge Photo: Tony Wheeler; Signs point the way Photo: Richard I'Anson

WHERE
The 610-kilometre Oodnadatta Track links Marree to Marla via Oodnadatta in northern South Australia.

WHEN
The Oodnadatta Cup, a local horse race, is held on Adelaide Cup Day in May. The Marree Picnic Races, held on the Queen's Birthday weekend in June, attract a good crowd. Also popular is the Marree Australian Camel Cup, held on the first Saturday in July on odd-numbered years.

HOW
The track is a good road by outback standards and usually suitable for robust conventional vehicles with strong suspension and good ground clearance.

Entry to the conservation areas of outback South Australia requires a Desert Parks Pass (call the Desert Parks Hotline on 1800 816 078). If you're just visiting Lake Eyre overnight, you'll need a day/night permit. Passes can be bought at various Department for Environment and Heritage (DEH; 08-8204 1910) or National Parks offices throughout South Australia.

The Aboriginal-owned and operated Arabunna Centre (08-8675 8351) in Marree runs a five-day camping tour of Arabunna country. Explore the Outback Camel Safaris (1800 064 244) does camel treks from William Creek. Wrightsair (08-8670 7962) flies over Lake Eyre from William Creek. Central Air Services (08-8675 8352), in Marree, offers flights over the Marree Man and parts of Lake Eyre.

Watch out for the opal bug **Photo:** Ross Barnett

Opals & Moon Plains: Coober Pedy Area

Coober Pedy is what you might call a unique town. As you roll towards it on the Stuart Highway, the blinding white desert is a pockmarked moonscape. The endless hillocks are opal mines – reputedly more than a million in the area. Glimmering opals were unearthed here in 1915, establishing the town as a mining mecca. The name Coober Pedy comes from the Aboriginal words *kupaka* (white man) and *piti* (hole), referring to the mines and subterranean dugouts many locals live in. The surrounding country is utterly desolate, the perfectly ruinous set for films such as *Mad Max III*, *Stark* and *Priscilla, Queen of the Desert*. Coober Pedy, however, does its best to distance itself from the apocalypse and, with more than forty nationalities present, is surprisingly cosmopolitan.

There are plenty of attractions, ranging from the informative to the weird and wacky. The 'Big Winch' lookout

dominates the town's skyline and has an appropriately shiny opal display. The Umoona Opal Mine & Museum has illuminating displays about local Aboriginal heritage. Under the same roof, the Aboriginal Interpretative Centre features a typical *wiltja* (mulga-tree shelter) and audio-visual displays about Dreaming stories. The Old Timers Mine and Crocodile Harry's dugout home – filled with the most amazing collection of junk and ephemera – are also worth a look.

You can't visit Coober Pedy without trying your hand at fossicking (or 'noodling') for opal chips – you never know what you'll find. Noodling in South Australia doesn't require a permit, but you should obtain permission from the landowner or holder of a registered claim before you start sifting. Another essential experience is spending the night in a dugout motel, where the temperature is regulated from

Conical tailings from mines and dugout villas dot the landscape **Photo:** Diana Mayfield

The Breakaways loom large near Coober Pedy **Photo:** Richard I'Anson

WHERE
Coober Pedy is on the Stuart Highway in South Australia, 539 kilometres north of Port Augusta and 688 kilometres south of Alice Springs.

WHEN
Outback South Australia is sizzlingly hot – no wonder everybody lives under-ground. Come during the cool winter months to dodge the heat. The Coober Pedy Opal Festival happens every Easter Saturday. The Coober Pedy Races, held on the Labour Day weekend (October) transform the locals into frenzied punters.

HOW
While no longer a true outback track now that it's sealed and well served by roadhouses, the 2700-kilometre Stuart Highway does go straight through the heart of outback Australia. From Coober Pedy to Glendambo (251 kilometres southeast), the highway cuts right through the Woomera Prohibited Area. Travelling off the main road into this area without a permit from the area administrator in Woomera is forbidden.

Most Coober Pedy tour operators aren't indigenous owned or run, but generally include the Breakaways and the Aboriginal Interpre-tative Centre. Try Radeka Breakaway Tours (08-8672 5223), Oasis Tours (08-8672 5169) or Desert Cave Tours (08-8672 5688).

The helpful Coober Pedy Tourist Office (08-8672 5298) is on the main road through town.

desert extremes and the rock-hewn walls create their own rugged ambience.

North of town is the Breakaways Reserve (also known as the painted desert) – a stony desert that was once an inland sea and home to various Aboriginal tribes for millennia. The three significant landmarks are *papa* (two dogs), also called the Castle; *kalaya* (emu); and *ungkata* (frill-necked lizard).

The township of Woomera, 372 kilometres south of Coober Pedy, feels decidedly ghostly – a long way from its noisy heyday in the 1950s and 1960s when it was used to launch top-secret experimental British rockets. Check out the museum at the Woomera Heritage Centre.

Not an adventure sport, yet
Photo: John Hay

Menindee Lake fills during high flows in the Darling River **Photo:** Oliver Strewe

Red Soil & Fish Traps: Outback NSW

You don't have to travel to central Australia to experience red deserts and limitless horizons. The far west of New South Wales is as remote, rugged and sparsely populated as it gets. The area also contains some of Australia's great rivers, all with fascinating parts to play in Aboriginal culture.

About 800 kilometres northwest of Sydney, on the banks of the mighty and muddy Darling River, lies Bourke, most famous for the expression 'back of Bourke', which denotes anywhere remote. The grave of Dr Fred Hollows, an opthalmologist who did much to improve the health of indigenous peoples in Australia, is in the Bourke cemetery. While in and around Bourke you can tune into 2CUZ FM (106.5 MHz), which is run by the Muda Aboriginal Corporation.

The town of Brewarrina is on the banks of the Barwon-Darling River, east of Bourke. The Ngunnhu, a series of

stone traps where for countless generations the Ngiyampaa people have caught fish to feed huge annual intergroup gatherings, create a fascinating diversion here. Despite industrial quarrying, these traps are still in use today. In summer, you may be able to buy a freshly caught fish from a local and have yourself a fish feast. Nearby, the Brewarrina Aboriginal Cultural Museum is a fine place to get a sense of both bush and mission life. In the early 1900s Aboriginal families from sixteen language groups were forcefully relocated to the Brewarrina Mission and made to share cramped quarters, with no sensitivity given to their cultural needs. Other tragic things have happened here, too. In 1987 Lloyd Boney, a local Aboriginal football hero, was found hanging by a sock in his jail cell just an hour after he was incarcerated. The ensuing riots by outraged locals resulted in the 1991 Royal Commission into Aboriginal Deaths in Custody.

Kangaroos thrive on the grasslands of outback New South Wales **Photo:** Mitch Reardon

Storm clouds ahead **Photo:** Gary Steer

Mount Gundabooka, between Bourke and Cobar, is of spiritual significance to local Aborigines and features exquisite cave paintings, including depictions of the Brewarrina fish traps and Biame (a Creator spirit). At Byrock, south of Bourke on the Mitchell Highway, you can see an ancient water hole that Biame made by digging the rock with his stone axe.

Northwest of Cobar, Mount Grenfell Historic Site protects over 1300 Aboriginal cave paintings. The park was handed back to the Ngiyampaa Wangaaypuwan people in 2004. The five-kilometre three-hour Ngiyampaa Walk takes you to the top of the ridge for a fabulous view of the Cobar Pediplain, where the Ngiyampaa Wangaaypuwan lived, hunted and foraged for centuries.

The wedge-tailed eagle, Australia's largest living bird of prey, is king of the skies in these parts
Photo: Oliver Strewe

WHERE

This wedge of far west New South Wales roughly covers the area west of the Castlereagh Highway to just east of the Mitchell Highway, with the Oxley and Barrier Highways forming the southern boundary.

WHEN

The best time to visit is during autumn or spring, when you'll avoid excessively hot or cold weather.

HOW

The roads are mostly in good condition and require no specific travel preparation. Bourke's tourist Information Centre (02-6872 2280) has the *Back O' Bourke Mud Map Tours* leaflet, which details drives to places of indigenous interest.

The Brewarrina Museum (02-6839 2628) runs Walkabout Tours that include camping under the stars and listening to Dreaming stories around the campfire while preparing and eating bush tucker.

Before heading out to Mount Gundabooka, book entry at the tourist office in Bourke. The Department of Environment and Conservation (DEC) in Bourke (02-6872 2744) occasionally provides guided tours in the July school holidays. Inquire at the DEC in Cobar about tours of Mount Grenfell with Ngiyampaa Wangaaypuwan guides.

A lonely windmill punctuates the empty horizon **Photo:** Cheryl Conlon

Hearths & Burial Sites: Silver City Hwy

For those travelling north from Melbourne, the Silver City Highway is one of the best introductions to the vastness and uniqueness of the Australian outback. If you are journeying west from Sydney or east from Adelaide, the Silver City Highway cuts across your course – you will probably meet it at the outback mining town of Broken Hill (also known as Silver City), from which the highway gains its name.

Although the expansive desert landscape is the main attraction in these parts, Broken Hill itself is worth a stop. Street names such as Chloride, Bromide and Sulphide add a bit of quirkiness, as do pieces of abandoned mining machinery amid the gold-boom architecture. The Broken Hill City Art Gallery features a permanent display of Aboriginal art, and the Thankakali Aboriginal Cultural Centre houses an impressive number of reasonably priced paintings and carvings.

Northeast of Broken Hill is the rugged Mutawintji National Park. Rock carvings, cave art and artefacts indicate that for over 8000 years the area was populated by various tribes, all attracted by rock holes permanently full of water. The park was returned to the traditional owners in 1998, and is now held by the Mutawintji Local Aboriginal Land Council on behalf of its Aboriginal owners and leased back to the Department of Environment and Conservation (DEC). Its network of trails and guided walks led by Aboriginal rangers make for an enriching experience.

Part of the World Heritage–listed Willandra Lakes Region, Lake Mungo is the site of the most significant archaeological finds in Australia: human skeletons and artefacts that date back 46,000 years (and possibly up to 60,000). These finds reveal that Aborigines settled by fertile lakes here, although the lakes dried up about 15,000 years ago, and a

Mural on the Maari Ma Health Aboriginal Corporation, Broken Hill **Photo:** Ross Barnett

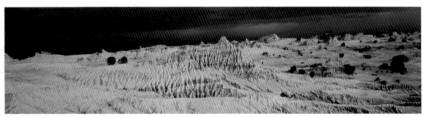

The eroded Walls of China in Mungo National Park **Photo:** Richard I'Anson

WHERE
Starting on the New South Wales side of the Murray, near Mildura, Silver City Highway stretches 679 kilometres to the New South Wales–Queensland border. The main town along the route is Broken Hill (New South Wales), 1200 kilometres west of Sydney and 900 kilometres north of Melbourne.

WHEN
Rainfall is spread fairly evenly throughout the year but is usually heaviest in June, so perhaps avoid this time of year if you're heading for the dirt section of the highway north of Broken Hill. Summer temperatures are mostly in the low thirties but because of the low humidity are fairly bearable.

HOW
North of Tibooburra, the road is remote and pure dirt to Warri Warri Gate on the New South Wales–Queensland border, 393 kilometres north of Broken Hill. The *Indian Pacific* choofs its way from Sydney to Broken Hill on Monday and Thursday.

Mutawintji Heritage Tours (08-8088 7000) has Mutawintji-run tours of the park. These include the Mutawintji Historic Site – off-limits unless you're on a tour. In most school holidays the Department of Environment and Conservation in Broken Hill (08-8088 3200) runs Discovery programmes, hosted by Aboriginal guides, to Mutawintji and Mungo National Parks. Jumbunna Walkabout Tours (0412 581 699) and Ponde Tours (03-5023 2488) are Aboriginal operators visiting Mungo National Park.

harsh semidesert environment prevailed. A twenty-five-kilometre semicircle (lunette) of huge sand dunes has been created by the unceasing westerly wind, which continually exposes fabulously ancient remains of hearths and burial sites. These shimmering white dunes are poetically known as the Walls of China and their story traces that of humans in Australia. These days, local Aboriginal communities are strongly involved in the preservation of the park and act as tour operators and guides.

Tibooburra, north of Broken Hill on the perimeter of Sturt National Park, is a cute little gold-rush town with granite rock formations on its outskirts. The Tibooburra Local Aboriginal Land Council Keeping Place displays artefacts from the Wadigali, Wongkumara and Malyangapa tribes.

Hand stencils at Amphitheatre Gorge in Mutawintji National Park
Photo: Ross Barnett

Early morning on the empty Nullarbor **Photo:** Denis O'Byrne

A Long, Lonely Road: Nullarbor Plain

Ask most Australians what they think the ultimate road trip is and they'll reverently answer 'Crossing the Nullarbor'. The Eyre Highway between Ceduna, South Australia, and Norseman, Western Australia, is the route, but this long, lonely road only briefly crosses the southern edge of the vast Nullarbor Plain. The highway's namesake was explorer Edward John Eyre, the first white man to make the east–west crossing in 1841. It wasn't until 1976 that the last stretch of his route was sealed.

Steeped in Wirangu Aboriginal history, the Nullarbor (Latin for 'no trees') is an enormous, stony plain with some amazing underground cave systems. Heading west, Ceduna (Wirangu for 'resting place') is the last sizable town until Norseman. After passing Fowlers Bay and the legendary surf at Cactus Beach, the road runs through Yalata Aboriginal land then enters the 5930-square-kilometre Nullarbor

National Park, paralleling the utterly photogenic Bunda Cliffs on the Great Australian Bight. The Yalata community consists of predominantly southern Pitjantjatjara and Kokatha people, resettled from Maralinga (see below). The road swings inland to Norseman, passing the Nuytsland Nature Reserve and Newman Rock. The Yalata people would gather in great numbers at Murrawijinie Cave and sing to commune with whales. Temperatures inside the caves can be over ten degrees cooler than above-ground temperatures. Today hawks and swallows nest in the caves – as do snakes, so take care!

Maralinga, an Aboriginal word for thunder, is on the northern edge of the Nullarbor. The British exploded atomic bombs here in 1956 and 1957 and conducted plutonium 'safety tests' between 1960 and 1963. Prior to detonation, most of the area's nomadic Aborigines were moved to

Galloping camels may cross your path Photo: Richard Nebesky

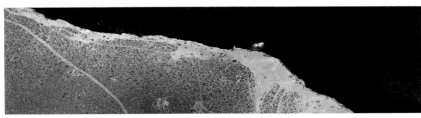

Where the desert meets the sea Photo: Diana Mayfield

Yalata, but in the mid-1980s, health concerns prompted a Commission of Enquiry. It found the local people had suffered greatly due to the tests, that the bomb sites were still contaminated and suggested it was Britain's responsibility to mop up the mess. Finally, in 1998, a $104 million operation (forty per cent funded by the British government) cleaned up a lot of contamination.

Between June and October, southern right whales visit the Great Australian Bight to breed or give birth. The best spot (on land) to watch these awesome creatures is the Head of Bight on Yalata Aboriginal land. Whales feature in Dreaming stories, and the occasional beached beast was used by the Wirangu for food and implements.

Waiting for the train in Watson
Photo: Ulrike Welsch

WHERE
The Nullarbor Plain stretches for 600 kilometres on either side of the Western and South Australian border, above the Great Australian Bight.

WHEN
Visit in winter or early spring to watch southern right whales in the Bight.

HOW
Driving from Ceduna to Norseman (1219 kilometres) takes three days including sightseeing. Adelaide to Ceduna is 761 kilometres and Norseman to Perth is 721 kilometres: 2701 kilometres in all and a five-day drive. The longest distance between fuel stops on the Eyre Highway is 188 kilometres – you shouldn't run out of petrol, but make sure your vehicle is in good shape and take plenty of drinking water. The long straight road tempts you to put the foot down, but you're a long way from hospital and plenty of big roos are waiting to mess up your car, especially at night.

The Ceduna Visitors Centre (1800 639 413) and Norseman Tourist Bureau (08-9039 1071) brim with information. Permits aren't required on the Eyre, even though it crosses Yalata Aboriginal land. Get whale-watching permits from the Ceduna Visitors Centre. Camping in Nullarbor National Park or Nullarbor Regional Reserve also requires a permit – contact the administrative officer at the Ceduna Department for the Environment and Heritage (08-8625 3144/2946 for Maralinga-Tjarutja Aboriginal land permits).

It's about getting in there people up here is they're so tea with you and share their and talking willing stories

Ngaanyatjarra kids from Warburton pause in their play for the camera Photo: Oliver Strewe

Art & History: Warburton Area

The names of the various roads and landmarks around the remote town of Warburton tell a fascinating tale. Back in 1873 this region saw a flurry of activity when three explorers vied for the honour of discovering what lay between the Overland Telegraph Line and the Western Australian coast.

William Gosse headed southwest from Alice Springs and he and his men eventually became the first whites to see Uluru (p88), which Gosse named Ayers Rock. Around the same time, Ernest Giles had seen from a distance a cluster of rounded peaks (the highest of which he called Mount Olga); however, Gosse beat him to Kata Tjuta (the Olgas; p88) by four weeks. Giles explored and named the spectacular Petermann Ranges, and from here continued his push westward, taking with him a young stockman by the name of Alf Gibson. When Gibson's horse broke down, Giles gave him his own horse and, knowing it was impossible to con-

tinue, sent Gibson back to bring help from their base camp. Gibson never made it. Giles, alone and on foot, with hardly a drop of water, did. Arriving at Circus Water, he drank his fill and came upon a dying wallaby. 'I pounced upon it and ate it, living, raw, dying – fur, skin, bones, skull and all', he later wrote. Giles named the Gibson Desert in memory of the stockman. He returned to civilisation only to find he had been beaten in his quest for the west by Major Peter Warburton. Warburton had pushed northwest from Alice Springs, finally making it to the coast north of present-day Port Hedland despite having almost died in the attempt.

By 1900 the gold rush was on, and prospectors explored the region along the Petermann Ranges. One was Harold Lasseter, whose fabulous lost reef of gold became the stuff of legend. Many prospectors have since attempted to locate his fabled reef, but to no avail.

o people. The great thing about the
talk, sit down and have a cup of
and tales from the land. — Deb

The 1950s brought the construction of the Woomera Rocket Range (p101) and the Emu and Maralinga (p106) atomic test sites, along with a series of desert highways known as the Bomb Roads. The Gunbarrel Highway (as in 'straight as') was the first to run east–west across central Australia and, for better or worse, ushered the modern world in to this ancient landscape.

Today the Giles weather station is used to amass information for weather forecasts and for, but its original purpose was to ensure that the days chosen for the big bangs at the atomic test sites were perfect and that the wind was blowing in the right direction. With advance permission you can catch the launching of the weather balloon at 8.45am (kids love it). You can also view the high-tech control room and decidedly low-tech measuring field, as well as a grader used by the Gunbarrel Road Construction Party and the remains of a rocket fired from Woomera.

Another worthwhile attraction is the impressive Tjulyuru Cultural & Civic Centre, just north of the town of Warburton. Initiated in a spirit of self-determination, the centre has exquisite artworks from the local Ngaanyatjarra community. Over 300 pieces from the nationally prized Aboriginal-owned Warburton Arts collection are on display.

Below, from top: Ngaanyatjarra elder; Driving the road between Warburton and Docker River **Photos:** Oliver Strewe

WHERE
Warburton is in Western Australia, 566 kilometres west of Yulara and about 900 kilometres north of Kalgoorlie.

WHEN
June to October is the best time to travel in this area.

HOW
The major routes through this region are the Great Central Road and the Gunbarrel Highway, which run west from Yulara (near Uluru) to Wiluna to meet the Canning Stock Route (p110). The Great Central Road is a well-maintained dirt highway, but the Gunbarrel section is a rough, remote track that passes through beautiful parts of the Gibson Desert.

To travel the Gunbarrel Highway and Great Central Road you will need permits from the Central Land Council in Alice Springs (08-8951 6320) and Western Australia (08-9235 8058), and from the Ngaanyatjarra Council (08-8950 1711), which together cover the area between Warbuton and Yulara.

Ossies Outback Tours (03-5222 2855) includes the entire route as part of a longer safari that takes in the Canning Stock Route and Tanami Track. Global Gypsies (08-9341 6727) traverses the Great Central Road section as part of its Perth to Alice Springs itineraries. Ossies Outback Tours and Global Gypsies also allow you to tag along with your own vehicle.

All smiles at Wirrimanu (Balgo) **Photo:** Peter Hendrie

Wells, Water Holes & Wildflowers: Canning Stock Route

The Canning Stock Route (CSR), the longest stock route in the world, crosses the Little Sandy Desert, the Gibson Desert, the Great Sandy Desert and, in its northern part, the western section of the Tanami Desert. The CSR (also known as Warntarri Purlumanupurru) passes through the territory of at least ten Aboriginal nations. Some fifty-four wells and water holes dot the route.

Along the route you can find evidence of Aboriginal occupation, particularly in the stone country where there are greater numbers of semipermanent water holes. Camping places are quite common, with stone scatters further emphasising Aboriginal occupation. The ancient practice of firestick farming (controlled burning to prevent uncontrolled bushfires) was used in the area to promote new growth and encourage greater animal numbers. There is rock art at Biella Spring – very clear ochre paintings of what appear to

be men surrounded by snakes – and at Canning's Cairn and Killagurra Springs.

With luck, your trip up the Canning will coincide with rain somewhere along its course. The chances of that happening are pretty good, as the stock route traverses such a vast segment of land. The occasional rainstorm brings with it an unexpected bounty of flowers, including acacias, grevilleas, hakeas, cassia, *mulla mulla* (pussy tails) and daisies. Special treats include the delicate, star-shaped, pink flower of the desert-fringe myrtle and the yellow-green, bird-shaped flower of the parrot-pea bush.

Approaching Durba Hills from the south in the evening is an unforgettable experience, as the rugged escarpment glows fiery red in the rays of the setting sun. Durba Springs is a place not to miss: you can explore the head of the gorge

Wind ruffles a clump of spinifex grass **Photo:** Peter Ptschelinzew

A sand ridge emerges from a sea of spinifex grass **Photo:** Diana Mayfield

WHERE
The Canning Stock Route
(CSR) runs 1700 kilome-
tres southwest from Halls
Creek (2977 kilometres
northeast of Perth) to
Wiluna (950 kilometres
northeast of Perth), in
Western Australia.

WHEN
June to September are the
best times to travel. Outside these times, expect
extreme heat, isolation
and potentially boggy
conditions.

HOW
This is the most difficult
four-wheel-drive route in
Australia; you must travel
in a well-equipped party,
and careful navigation is
required. If you wish to
travel to any of the outlying
communities, contact the
Kimberley Land Council
(08-9193 1118).

BikeRoundOz (info@bike
roundoz.com) runs enduro-
style motorcycle trips along
the route. Several outfits
provide four-wheel-drive
trips to the area, including Great Divide Tours
(02-9913 1395), Direct
4WD (08-8952 3359) and
Exprim Tours (www.exprim
.com.au).

and the surrounding country, and there are many Aboriginal art sites within the nearby hills and gorges. It is also a
haven for birds.

In Walmajarri country, the Billiluna-Mindibung Aboriginal
community at the northern end of Lake Gregory has a cultural centre with displays of historical records and artefacts,
and arts and crafts for sale. The world-renowned Warlayirti
Artists Aboriginal Corporation at Wirrimanu (Balgo) promotes over 200 artists whose work can be viewed at their
art centre. Their paintings reflect the traditional stories of
their homelands, and these painters are renowned for their
vibrant colours and highly expressive work.

The complex rock carvings at Punda Photo: Peter Ptschelinzew

Oases & Songlines: The Pilbara

The Pilbara region encompasses some of the hottest country on earth. It also contains the iron ore that accounts for much of Western Australia's prosperity. Gigantic machines are used to tear apart the dusty red ranges of this isolated, harsh and fabulously wealthy area. The Pilbara towns are almost all company towns: either mining centres where the ore is wrenched from the earth or ports from which it's shipped abroad. The surrounding arid areas and mountain ranges are an ancient, raw frontier full of majesty and contrast.

At Weeli Wolli, crystal-clear springs and waterfalls flow for about five kilometres. Tall paperbark trees and river gums tower over the water, and there are even some date palms. The area is also rich in fish and bird life. The water holes are accessible by four-wheel drive from Newman, the region's largest town.

There's no doubt that the ancient Hamersley Range, with some of the oldest rock formations in the world dating back four billion years, contains some of Australia's most dramatic scenery. The landscape is dotted with spectacular red gorges, occasional waterfalls and palm-fringed water holes. It's a land synonymous with the Dreaming and abounds in Aboriginal sites. Eroded forms of prehistory are overlaid with the machinery of modern explorers in search of abundant raw materials and minerals.

The Western Pilbara is the home of the Martu people, who are split into many different language groups. The Wanna Munna Protected Area rock-art carvings feature images of humans, animals and water symbols. The Punda rock carvings, depicting animals and people with boomerangs among other things, cover an isolated hillside. There is also a deep rock hole filled with cool water near the rock carvings. If

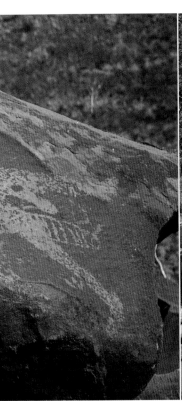

The river at the base of Dales Gorge, Karijini National Park Photo: Diana Mayfield

WHERE
The Pilbara is in Western
Australia. Newman, the
region's main town, is
1186 kilometres northeast
of Perth.

WHEN
From October to April the
temperature reaches or
exceeds thirty-two degrees
Celsius almost every day.
During winter the maximum
temperature usually hovers
around a more tolerable
twenty-five degrees Celsius.

HOW
Roads are generally good
and are regularly graded,
but unless you are an
experienced and skilled
four-wheel-drive user do
not attempt to travel out to
Wanna Munna or Punda.
Permits are not required
for Punda but visitors are
discouraged. For more
information contact the
Newman Information
Centre (08-9175 2888).
The Department of Conser-
vation & Land Management
(CALM) website (www.calm
.wa.gov.au) offers tips for
remaining safe in these
remote areas.

Contact the Western
Desert Puntukurnuparna
Aboriginal Corporation
(WDPAC; 08-9172 3299)
if you wish to visit any of
the Martu communities
independently. You can
take a tour to the rock-art
sites with Joe and Maria
Furulyas (08-9175 1715)
on a Pilbara Iron Country
Tag-a-long tour. You will
need to provide your own
food and supplies and an
off-road four-wheel drive
for the day. There are easy
day tours or full-day tours
for moderate/experienced
drivers.

you walk up the gorge from the rock hole you'll find clear
pools filled with fish, as well as colourful water-worn rocks.

One of the most isolated national parks in Australia, the
15,000-square-kilometre Rudall River National Park
(originally known as Karlamilyi) has an almost merciless
grandeur about it. With its permanent water supply, it is
considered an oasis. Occupied by the Wanman, Mandjild-
jarra, Ngolibardu and Gardutjarra groups, the park has some
great stories involving songlines (also known as Dreaming
tracks), which follow the journey of the Spirit Ancestors as
they sang up the country into life. Within the park, Lake
Dora is the place where two Creator Being snakes disappeared underground, and so the mouth of the lake (near
Lake Blanche) holds special significance. South of Lake
Dora is Lake Disappointment, a salt lake that is a taboo
area. It offers little in terms of resources for living and is
best avoided anyway due to the fearful Ngayurnangalku
beings that live underneath the lake. They are said to be
capable of pulling aircraft from the sky and forcing them to
crash on the lake's surface. You have been warned!

A Nyabalee man cooks emu on the fire
near Newman Photo: Peter Ptschelinzew

113

Tropical

A beautifully patterned whale shark stalked by a snorkeller **Photo:** Michael Aw

Treasures of the Reef:
Coral Coast

Extending from Coral Bay to Onslow, the Coral Coast is home to the stunning Ningaloo Reef, Western Australia's answer to the Great Barrier Reef. The reef stretches 250 kilometres off the coast and is amazingly accessible, with some parts lying just 100 metres offshore.

With over 220 recorded species of coral, the reef attracts the area's other claim to fame: the whale shark, the largest fish in the world. Whale sharks can weigh up to twenty-one tonnes, and reach up to eighteen metres long. These gentle giants arrive like clockwork each year to feed on plankton and small fish. Ningaloo is the only place in the world where these creatures reliably appear each year, making it a mecca for marine biologists and visitors alike. There are also more than 500 species of fish, including sharks and manta rays, as well as humpback whales, turtles and dugongs. Coral Bay is a tiny community nestled at the edge

of a picturesque bay at the southern end of Ningaloo Reef. Enclosing the bay is a protective reef that provides good snorkelling within spitting distance of the shore.

On the west side of the North West Cape (the finger of land that runs alongside the reef) is Cape Range National Park, a spectacular landscape of canyons, pristine beaches and limestone ranges. There are over 700 caves in the ranges, which were well used by Aboriginal communities. The caves offer shelter close to the abundant food resources of the reef, and this area has huge archaeological importance. There are short walks to Mandu Mandu Gorge and Yardie Creek in the park's far south.

The remains of a meal of shellfish from around 30,000 years ago, found on the North West Cape, are Australia's oldest evidence of a seafood dinner. But the discovery that

Clear waters lap the shore at Turquoise Bay, Ningaloo Marine Park **Photo:** Claver Carroll

Sheer walls and still waters at Yardie Creek Gorge, Cape Range National Park **Photo:** Paul Harding

most excited archaeologists was a 32,000-year-old shell necklace found in a Mandu Mandu rock shelter in 1990. This necklace, now held by the Western Australian Museum, is one of the oldest known examples of human ornamentation found anywhere in the world.

A dugong comes up for air **Photo:** Jason Edwards

WHERE
The Coral Coast extends from Coral Bay to Onslow, midway up Western Australia's coast.

WHEN
The high season lasts from April to October, but there's always something happening on the reef. From March to May there's coral spawning, from March to June you can see whale sharks and from June to November there are manta rays. Every June and July humpback whales pass close by the coast on the way north to their calving grounds; they return in October and November on their way to Antarctica. Finally, from November to March it's turtle-nesting and -hatching season.

HOW
Cape Range National Park is easily accessible by car or the Ningaloo Reef Bus (1800 999 941). For information contact the Department of Conservation & Land Management (CALM; 08-9949 1676) in Exmouth.

If you want to see whale sharks, tours operate out of both Exmouth (up to eight boats) and Coral Bay (two boats). Outside the whale-shark season, half-day manta-ray tours and dive trips and courses are also available.

Striding through Roebourne **Photo:** Peter Ptschelinzew

Ice-Age Rock Art: Coastal Pilbara

The Pilbara (meaning 'freshwater fish') is a working region – a vast arid land with a heart of iron-ore, offering a fascinating insight into the heavy industry of the outback. The coastal section of the Pilbara extends from Onslow to Port Hedland and inland beyond the Millstream-Chichester National Park. Company towns built to mine and ship the ore form the infrastructure of the region, but the Pilbara's rich Aboriginal heritage can be seen at many important sites.

In Karratha, the Jaburara Heritage Trail is a self-guided walk highlighting 5000-year-old rock engravings, grinding stones, etchings and middens. Jaburara (pronounced 'yabura') is the name of the traditional owners of the Karratha region. The *thalu* (a ceremonial site to encourage the generation of a species) that features on the trail is related to the Warramurrangka (Giant Fruit Bat) and forms the mythical path of this spiritual being.

Nearby, the Murujuga rock-art site on the Burrup Peninsula is one of the largest rock-art galleries in the world and a major international heritage site. It contains 10,000 Aboriginal rock engravings depicting fish, turtles, euros (wallaroos), wallabies and the Tasmanian tiger. Crystal-erosion dating, which measures the erosion rate of exposed crystals in the rock, has dated these etchings at 27,000 years, around the time of the last ice age. This area also has the largest occurrence of standing stones (similar to Europe's megaliths) in Australia.

East of Karratha, Roebourne is home to a large Aboriginal community. For a good introduction to Aboriginal heritage, visit the Roebourne Tourist Bureau or Cossack, just west of Roebourne, for the Cheeditha Aboriginal Gallery in the old Galbraith Store (1890). Port Hedland, the other major town in the region, features Aboriginal displays at the Dalgety House Museum and Courthouse Arts Centre & Gallery.

Rocky landscape dotted with termite mounds on the road to Millstream-Chichester National Park **Photo:** Peter Ptschelinzew

When it's time for a swim, head out to the cool water holes of the Fortescue River in Millstream-Chichester National Park (Ngarrari). Occupying an area of 2200 square kilometres, the park is of great spiritual significance, with many references to the Dreaming. The Deep Reach Pool is the resting place for the Great Snake, the protector of the waters in the area. The Chinderwarriner Pool, featuring shady palms and lilies, was also an important meeting area for local clans.

The former Millstream homestead forms the visitors centre, with interpretive displays on the lifestyle of the Yinjibarndi people. There are plenty of good walking trails in the park – try the Murlunmunyjurna Trail, which features river crossings over palm-trunk bridges and interpretive information on Yinjibarndi plants.

Water lilies blanket a river
Photo: Peter Ptschelinzew

WHERE
The Pilbara is a vast area occupying the hump of Western Australia; the coastal region in the north stretches along the Indian Ocean. For information on the rest of the Pilbara, see p112.

WHEN
With average summer temperatures of forty-one degrees Celsius, the Pilbara town of Marble Bar is known as the hottest place in Australia, and many prefer to visit the region in the winter months (June to August), when temperatures average around twenty-seven degrees Celsius. Cyclone season is from 1 November to 30 April.

HOW
Roads are well maintained in the Pilbara and fairly accessible by four-wheel drive. Millstream-Chichester National Park is accessed via a dirt road, so check road conditions at the tourist bureau before setting off. Karratha Visitors Centre (08-9144 4600) sells *Jaburara Heritage Trail* brochures, and can help you find the engravings on the Burrup Peninsula. Roebourne Visitors Centre (08-9182 1060) can organise Aboriginal cultural experiences. Snappy Gum Safaris (08-9185 2141) has day trips to Millstream-Chichester.

The extraordinary striped rock stacks of the towering Bungle Bungles **Photo:** Oliver Strewe

Domes & Ravines:
Purnululu National Park Region

The beehive formations of the Bungle Bungle massif, in Purnululu National Park, are an amazing spectacle: impressive rounded sandstone towers with an exterior crust striped in bands of orange and blackish-green. They are rated by many as the top scenic wonder of Western Australia.

Traditionally the land of the Kija and Djaru people, who still live in settlements in the east Kimberley, Purnululu (the Kija word for sandstone) contains Aboriginal art and a number of burial sites, though these are not accessible to the public. Secluded by distance and the surrounding ranges, the Bungles remained hidden from prying eyes until 1982. Previously known only to a few drovers, helicopter pilots and local Aboriginal people, the area became an instant hit when it was featured in a television documentary on the scenic wonders of Western Australia. In March 1987, Purnululu National Park was gazetted. In 2003,

Purnululu National Park and the Bungle Bungle massif were declared a World Heritage site.

A walk to Cathedral Gorge, in the southern reaches of the park, arguably one of Australia's most sensational and awe-inspiring natural wonders, takes you past spectacular domes and along an ever-narrowing ravine. Suddenly, around a corner, it opens up into a large amphitheatre. The walls encroach on all sides, a smallish patch of sky adding to the grandeur of this magical place. This sight makes the trek, and all the dust, worthwhile. A much longer walk leads to the soaring Piccaninny Gorge, further northeast along the southern ramparts of the range.

Echidna Chasm, Frog Hole and Mini Palms in the north of the park are also well worth exploring. As you progress up Echidna Chasm, it becomes narrower and narrower as the

Phyllis Thomas, from the Juwulinypany community, works on a painting inspired by the Bungle Bungles **Photo:** Richard I'Anson

WHERE
Purnululu National Park is in Western Australia, 109 kilometres north of Halls Creek, off the Great Northern Highway.

WHEN
The park is closed during the Wet, from 1 January to 31 March, but earlier or later rains can still make the access track impassable. During the Dry temperatures are almost freezing at night.

HOW
The road into the national park is a rough, dusty and tedious four-wheel-drive track with a few tricky creek crossings that can be deep in water.

To visit the Kelarriny-Warmun Arts Centre (08-9168 7496), call first for permission to enter the community.

Opposite the Turkey Creek Roadhouse in Warmun, the Daiwul Gidja Cultural Centre offers half- and full-day bush tours as well as a two-day Aboriginal cross-cultural awareness course that is accredited nationally. Discover the Kimberley Tours (1800 636 802) runs four-wheel-drive and helicopter trips to the park. Bungle Bungle Adventures (1800 641 998) arranges two- and three-day backpacker safari tours.

walls close in. Finally, it is just an arm-span wide and towers well over 100 metres upwards. It is a spectacular place.

There are also a few interesting places to visit in the area surrounding the park. At Warmun (Turkey Creek), north of Purnululu, you can visit the Kelarriny-Warmun Arts Centre. Warmun artists are renowned for their distinctive work, which embodies traditional and contemporary Kija culture. Northwest of Purnululu is the Lumuku Aboriginal Corporation, also known as Osmond Valley. This tropical oasis on the fringe of Purnululu has fresh springs and various walking tracks. South of Purnululu, the 835-metre-wide and fifty-metre-deep Wolfe Creek Crater, originally known as Kandimala, is the second-largest known meteorite crater in the world. In the Dreaming, two Rainbow Serpents wove their way across the desert, leaving behind their prints in the form of riverbeds; one snake raised his head at Kandimala, leaving behind the crater.

Above, from top: Wolfe Creek Crater
Photo: Tony Wheeler
In amongst Echidna Chasm, Purnululu National Park **Photo:** Trevor Creighton

Celebrating after the big game **Photo:** John Borthwick

Fine Art & Footy Fever: Tiwi Islands

Threaded with pretty waterways and rainforest-lined swimming holes, this idyllic tropical island retreat is eighty kilometres north of Darwin in the Arafura Sea. Bathurst and Melville Islands are two large, flat islands owned by the Tiwi Aboriginal community. This is a corner of Australia that's off the tourist trail and well worth the effort to visit. You're guaranteed a fascinating insight into Islander life – starting with a relaxed welcome, a mug of billy tea and a slab of damper (bush bread cooked on an open fire).

Tiwi culture has always been quite distinct from the Aboriginal culture on the mainland. The Islanders are famous for two things – their beautiful and unusual *pukumani* (burial ceremonies) and their passion for football.

The biggest event on the island calendar is the Footy Grand Final. Aussie Rules football is an obsession among Tiwi

people (former Richmond star Maurice Rioli and his nephew Dean, who plays for Essendon, both come from Melville Island). The Grand Final in late March is a major event on the Northern Territory sporting calendar and attracts up to 12,000 fans. It's an experience you'll never forget, but if you want to see it you'll need to book well in advance.

During the rest of the year, many Tiwi Islanders turn their attention to art. Due to their isolation, they developed art forms – mainly sculpture – not found anywhere else in Australia. The *pukumani* burial rites are one of the main rituals of Tiwi religious life, and it is for these ceremonies that many of the artworks are created: *yimwalini* or *tunga* (bark baskets), spears and *tutini* (burial poles). These carved and painted poles, up to two-and-a-half metres long, represent features of the deceased person's life and are placed around the grave. They are carved in ironwood,

Modern art: a boldy painted tin shed **Photo:** John Borthwick

WHERE
The Tiwi Islands are a twelve-minute flight north of Darwin. There are two main islands, Bathurst and Melville Island, but most Islanders live on Bathurst.

WHEN
Generally, the best time to visit the Tiwi Islands is in the Dry (June to October), but many people go in late March to see the Grand Final. Permits are not required to visit Nguiu on this day, but it's important to plan flights well in advance.

HOW
The only practical way to visit the islands is by organised tour, as there is no public accommodation or transport on the islands, and otherwise permits are only issued if you have a reason to visit.

Visitors have a chance to see Tiwi artists at work on the islands – see www.tiwiart.com for more information.

Tiwi Tours, owned by the Tiwi Islanders, contracts Aussie Adventure (08-1800 811 633) to run the Tiwi Island tours. These are fascinating and worthwhile, though interaction with the local Tiwi community tends to be limited to your guides and the local workshops and showrooms. There is also an overnight tour staying at a private bush camp. Although one day is long enough to see the sights, the extended tour allows you to get a better experience of the people and culture. Other camping tours may also be available in future.

which is impossible for termites to bore through, and form an eerie yet beautiful memorial at burial sites on the islands.

A tour of Bathurst Island usually includes a visit to a *pukumani* site, as well as the chance to have lunch, tea and damper with Tiwi women. They will explain some of their crafts, and experiences of the mission days, and perform a short dance. You can also get in a swim at the water hole and a visit to the early Catholic mission buildings and the craft workshops where Islanders have been taking new directions in art.

In the last fifty years the Tiwi have been producing sculptured animals and birds, many of

A Tiwi grave site with *tutini* (burial poles)
Photo: Peter Ptschelinzew

(continued on p125)

Tiwi islander casting a wide net Photo: Peter Ptschelinzew

these being Creation ancestors. More recently, bark painting, textile design, sculpture, ceramics and print-making have become popular. The Bima Wear textile factory was set up in 1969 to employ Tiwi women, and today makes curtains, towels and other fabrics in distinctive designs. Bima designed and printed the vestments worn by Pope John Paul on his visit to the territory in 1987.

There's also a small museum in Bathurst's major centre, Nguiu, which features sections dedicated to Apupwankijimi (Tiwi Dreaming), mission heritage and Arrakili (Tiwi culture), and where you can learn more about burial ceremonies, Creation stories and the impressive wartime history of the islands.

The competitive Tiwi spirit you see at work on the footy field goes back a long way. Tiwi Islanders are the closest Austral-

ian community to Asia and they have long been the first port of call for unwelcome visitors from the north. The Tiwi generally had poor relations with the Makasar, who, from the seventeenth century, came from the island of Celebes (now Sulawesi) in search of trepang (sea cucumbers). The Islanders earned a fierce reputation that stayed with them right through the colonial era. There is also some evidence that the Portuguese raided the islands for slaves in the seventeenth century, which may explain the origins of this hostility.

Bathurst Island was also the first point in Australia to be attacked by the Japanese in World War II. During the war, the people of the Tiwi Islands played a significant role by capturing fallen Japanese bomber pilots, rescuing Allied pilots and guiding Allied vessels through dangerous waters.

Tiwi Art Network (08-8941 3593) operates art tours directed at art enthusiasts and collectors. The one-day tour visits Tiwi Design on Bathurst Island. Tours are organised on demand from Monday to Friday.

Munupi Sport Fishing (08-8978 3783) runs fishing trips from its comfortable set-up at Pirlangimpi on Melville Island, near the ruins of Fort Dundas. The trips include meals, fishing, accommodation and flights (from Darwin).

The Catholic church on Bathurst Island – a hub of community activities **Photo:** Peter Ptschelinzew

All adorned in traditional body paint **Photo:** John Borthwick

Coral amongst seashells at Smith Point on the Cobourg Peninsula **Photo:** Richard l'Anson

Wetland Habitat: Cobourg Peninsula

The far-flung wilderness of the Cobourg Peninsula includes the Aboriginal-owned Garig Gunak Barlu National Park (previously known as Cobourg Marine Park and Gurig National Park). The park is part of the Arnhem Land Aboriginal Reserve and one of the few areas of Arnhem Land that is not closed to independent travellers. This expanse of land and coastline is much more remote than Kakadu and you must be behind the wheel of a four-wheel drive to access and enjoy it.

The Cobourg Peninsula is on the Ramsar List of Wetlands of International Importance (an international treaty for the conservation and sustainable use of wetlands) as it is the habitat of a variety of waterfowl and other migratory birds, while the waters are home to dugongs and six species of turtle. You're also likely to spot a few introduced animals, such as Indonesian bantang cattle and Timor ponies, all of

which were imported by the British when they attempted to settle the Top End in the nineteenth century. The coastline here is beautiful, but unfortunately the water is unsuitable for swimming due to salties (saltwater crocodiles), sharks, stonefish and sea snakes.

One of the drawcards here is fishing off the coast in waters well known as some of the best in Australia. It's not really possible to explore the inland parts of the area as there are virtually no tracks within the park apart from the main access track, but you can still wander along the white sandy beaches.

The park is jointly managed by the local Aboriginal inhabitants and the Northern Territory's Parks and Wildlife Commission. Alcohol must not be consumed while travelling through Arnhem Land, but it's permitted beyond the en-

Beachcombing on the Cobourg Peninsula **Photo:** Richard I'Anson

trance to Garig Gunak Barlu. At Black Point (Algarlarlgarl) there is a rangers station and visitors centre, which doubles as an informative cultural centre detailing the Aboriginal, European and Makasar people, and the history of Victoria Settlement. No caravans or trailers are allowed into the park.

The failed colonial outpost of Victoria Settlement (Murrumurrdmulya) at Port Essington, founded in 1838 and abandoned eleven years later, is well worth a visit but accessible by boat only. Still visible among the ruins are various chimneys and wells, the powder magazine and parts of the hospital.

Pandanus streaming in the breeze
Photo: Peter Ptschelinzew

WHERE

The Cobourg Peninsula is in the Northern Territory, 570 kilometres northeast of Darwin by road.

WHEN

The Cobourg track is closed in the Wet (January to March), usually opening in early May. The best time to visit is during the Dry (April to September). The period from October to December sees rising temperatures and humidity levels and dramatic storms.

HOW

The 270-kilometre track (four-wheel drive only) to Black Point on the Cobourg Peninsula begins at Oenpelli (p128). The route passes through part of Arnhem Land and, as the Aboriginal owners here restrict the number of vehicles going through to twenty at any one time, you're advised to apply up to a year ahead for the necessary transit permit, which includes entry and camping fees for the Garig Gunak Barlu (contact the permits officer on 08-8999 4814). The journey takes four to six hours, and must be completed in one day, as it's not possible to stop overnight outside the park itself.

Boat trips to Victoria Settlement can be booked at the Gurig store (1800 000 871) at Black Point, where you can also hire a dinghy for fishing trips. Cape Don Lodge (08-8979 0263), at the northwestern tip of the peninsula, is accessible by aircraft only and offers guided fishing and wildlife tours as part of its accommodation package.

127

Pelicans adrift on a billabong near Oenpelli **Photo:** Peter Ptschelinzew

Dilly-Bag Babies: Oenpelli

Spectacularly located on the edge of a billabong teeming with bird life, the Aboriginal community of Oenpelli (also known as Gunbalanya) lies in the shadow of the black-rock monolith of Injalak Hill on the western frontier of Arnhem Land, the largest Aboriginal reserve in Australia.

The short drive to Oenpelli from the Border Store in Kakadu National Park (p138) is worth a trip in itself – brilliant green wetlands, spectacular escarpments and a crossing of the croc-infested, tidal and superbly misnamed East Alligator River set the tone.

Oenpelli began life as Paddy Cahill's station early in the twentieth century. Cahill was a jockey, buffalo-hunter and pastoralist involved in the territory's largely unsuccessful foray into dairy farming. In 1925 the station passed to the Church Missionary Society, and it stayed a mission until

self-determination in the 1970s. It now boasts a population of around 1000 people predominantly from the Kunwinjku clans and is the hub of some ten outstations that lie to the east.

Your first port of call in Oenpelli should be the Injalak Arts & Crafts Association centre, which began life twenty years ago as a screen-printing workshop in a small shed and has since blossomed into a successful nonprofit community enterprise representing about 200 local artists and weavers.

The arts centre is both a shopfront, an impromptu community centre and a workplace for artists producing traditional paintings on bark and paper, pandanus weavings, baskets, dilly bags, screen-printed fabrics and didjeridus. In the cool of the morning you'll find many artists are hard at work on the centre's verandas.

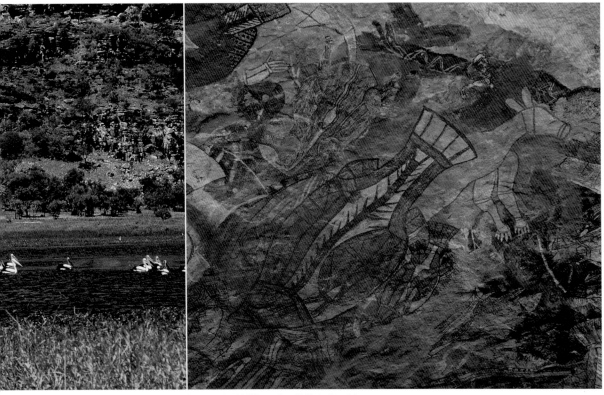

Rock art at Injalak Hill near Oenpelli **Photo:** Peter Solness

Modern Kunwinjku artists paint in the same X-ray style used by their forebears 8000 years ago in ancient rock art – visualising animals as if they could see right through the skin and depicting their skeletal framework. One way to get a sense of how this tradition continues unbroken across thousands of years is to arrange for a local guide to take you up Injalak Hill, where some of the finest rock-art galleries in Australia can be found.

It's a short, steep climb to the top – best done in the early morning before the heat of the day builds up – but it's well worth the effort, not only for the artwork in numerous caves and rock shelters but for the breathtaking panoramic views of the flood plains. As the Wet arrived each year and the rivers rose, Aboriginal families living on the fertile wetlands were forced to climb to higher ground on Injalak Hill, where they camped in caves and left their pictorial legacy.

Arnhem Land's lush vegetation **Photo:** Peter Solness

Kunwinjku kids flash past at Gunbalanya Community School. **Photo:** Peter Solness

Open-air assembly: the children of Gunbalanya Community School **Photo:** Peter Solness

The main gallery looks like a giant wall of graffiti, with dozens of human figures and animals layered one on top of another. The earliest images, perhaps as old as 50,000 years, show stick-thin ochre figures hunting; many others depict sources of food. Gradually, the subject matter expands to include myths and stories such as the Rainbow Serpent and the Dilly-Bag Lady who, according to legend, wandered across the country handing out babies in dilly bags, each baby representing a different language group in Arnhem Land.

Back at ground level, Oenpelli is home to the Karrabarrda Yam Dancers, an engaging dance troupe that celebrates the humble sweet potato – a traditional Kunwinjku staple of ceremonial significance. And it's also the regular stomping ground of a number of Arnhem Land's pluckiest rock bands, including Narbelek from outlying Manmoyi. These

musicians have creatively combined garage rock, native language and traditional stories in a bid to get young kids to listen to ancient lore.

Once a year Oenpelli holds a Cultural Open Day that showcases its art, music and dancing talents. It's a celebratory day with lots of bush tucker and some intertribal Aussie Rules Football. Permits are not required to visit the town on this day.

Arnhem Escarpment near Oenpelli overlooking Arnhem Land **Photo:** Peter Solness

Cath and Deb taking in the rock art at Injalak Hill near Oenpelli **Photo:** Peter Solness

WHERE

Oenpelli is in the Northern Territory, approximately 300 kilometres east of Darwin and seventeen kilometres east of the Border Store in Kakadu. The East Alligator River marks the boundary between Kakadu National Park and Arnhem Land.

WHEN

The town is accessible by road during the Dry (May to November) and by air only during the rest of the year. Check the tide times at the Bowali Visitor Centre (08-8938 1121) in Jabiru, in Kakadu, before crossing the East Alligator River, which can be impassable for a few hours either side of high tide at the start of the Dry. Oenpelli hosts its annual Open Day in August.

HOW

A permit is required to visit Oenpelli. Permits are issued by the Northern Land Council (www.nlc.org .au/html/permits.html) in Jabiru or Darwin and take at least twenty-four hours. The Injalak arts centre can organise guides for Injalak Hill.

If you're travelling independently, a four-wheel drive is strongly recommended. Alternatively, Arnhemlander Tours (08-8979 2411), run by the Djabulukgu Association, offers one-day four-wheel-drive trips from Jabiru in Kakadu. They visit the scenic Mikinj Valley near Oenpelli and include bush education, rock art and a visit to the Injalak arts centre.

Cath and Deb examine intricately decorated totem poles at the Buku-Larrngay Mulka Art Centre and Museum **Photo:** Peter Solness

Sunrise Country: Yirrkala

Perched on the tip of the Gove Peninsula, the tiny Aboriginal community of Yirrkala is one of the cultural strongholds of the Yolngu of northeastern Arnhem Land, arguably the most high-profile indigenous people in Australia. They have retained much of their traditional culture, and their way of life remains largely intact.

Locals such as Mandawuy and Galarrwuy Yunupingu (of the band Yothu Yindi, which had a string of hits in the 1980s and '90s), David Malangi (whose Aboriginal images appeared on Australia's first dollar note) and actor David Gulpilil have achieved national status.

With a population hovering just over 500, Yirrkala is a quiet, chilled-out kind of place, with most houses – including one designed by celebrated Australian architect Glenn Murcutt – strung out along the water's edge.

Aptly named after the feeling on your face when it is struck by the first rays of the sun, Yirrkala's Buku-Larrngay Mulka Art Centre & Museum is a major repository of bark painting, carved totems and weaving from the local community and surrounding outstations. Artists from this area – known as Miwatj (sunrise country) – have played a pivotal role in raising the profile and appreciation of Aboriginal art among nonindigenous people. The centre is one of the few places in Arnhem Land accessible to visitors without permission from traditional owners.

Pride of place in the centre goes to the two superb *Yirrkala Church Panels*, each measuring 1.2 metres by 3.6 metres and depicting one of the two moieties (skin classifications) underpinning the Yolngu kinship system: Dhuwa (the Lava of the Horned Beetle) and Yirritja (the Maggot). Everything in the Yolngu universe fits into one of these two classifications.

A wealth of information at the museum Photo: Peter Solness

The panels depict sacred designs and illustrate Yolngu connections and claims to the land and the sea – basically the Yolngu's native-title claim. Created in the early 1960s, they were hung in the local Methodist Mission Church until the 1970s, when a minister deemed them 'heathen'.

Also on display is a copy of the Yirrkala Bark Petition sent to the Australian Parliament in 1963 to protest the granting of a bauxite mining lease in Arnhem Land without Yolngu consultation. Although ultimately unsuccessful, the petition won the Yolngu some compensation and lay the groundwork for the Aboriginal Land Rights (NT) Act of 1976. As a result, Arnhem Land was returned to its original owners – a major turning point in the history of Aboriginal land rights.

The centre has one of the largest collections of Aboriginal art for sale in the Northern Territory, and includes bark paintings, *yidaki* (didjeridus) and unusual *larrakitj* (mortuary containers) – admittedly not the sort of thing you can just tuck under your arm and take on a plane, but freight can be arranged.

The annual Garma festival – established by the Yothu Yindi Foundation – takes place at Gulkula, near Yirrkala, each year. According to Yolngu law, this is where the Ancestor Ganbulabula brought the *yidaki* into being. Among Australia's most impressive indigenous festivals, Garma is dedicated to cultural exchange and the celebration of Yolngu dance, song, art and ceremony.

Below: The various attractions of Yirrkala Photos: Peter Solness

WHERE
Yirrkala is in northeastern Arnhem Land in the Northern Territory, approximately 600 kilometres east of Darwin and twenty kilometres southeast of Nhulunbuy.

WHEN
The Dry (between May and September) is the best time to visit. The Garma festival takes place in the first week of August.

HOW
You can fly into Nhulunbuy and visit the Buku-Larrngay Mulka Arts Centre & Museum in Yirrkala without a permit, but if you're planning to explore further afield you'll need to get permission from the Northern Land Council (www.nlc.org.au/html/permits.htm).

Nhulunbuy-based Birds, Bees, Trees & Things (08-8987 1814) is run by a nonindigenous local who works closely with Yolngu people running unstructured cultural tours in northeastern Arnhem Land.

Cath and a Yolngu woman preparing paperbark for use in Cath's bush sauna, involving burying her above a bed of roasting cycad nuts **Photo:** Peter Solness

The Trepang Trade:
Bawaka

On the far eastern tip of Arnhem Land's Gove Peninsula, Bawaka is an idyllic outstation looking out onto the turquoise waters of Port Bradshaw. Saltwater crocodiles notwithstanding, this is one place that undoubtedly qualifies for the status of tropical paradise. It's also a place of deep cultural wealth and pride – part of the heart and soul of Gumatj country.

Normally inaccessible to outsiders, Bawaka is the site of a recent indigenous tourism project that offers visitors the chance to immerse themselves in Yolngu family life and culture. There's nothing stage-managed about the activities here – this is about as organic as it gets. When you enter Bawaka, you enter Yolngu time – an unhurried, relaxing tempo where events unfold at their own pace.

Bawaka's residents are saltwater people, so it's a great place to learn about the Yolngu culture's profound connection to

the sea. The people in this neck of the woods were trading trepang (sea cucumbers) with Makasar – from the Indonesian island of Sulawesi – centuries before Captain Cook pulled on his sailing britches. Although trepang is poisonous in its natural state, it was valued by the Chinese as an aphrodisiac and effectively became Australia's first export industry.

From the sixteenth century, the Makasar took advantage of northwest monsoon winds to sail their *prahus* from Sulawesi to the coast of Arnhem Land. They stayed several months each year until the southeast winds returned, employing Yolngu to dive, gather and spear trepang in return for food, tobacco and knives.

The trade continued for at least three centuries and the ties between the cultures became strong with intermarriage. Many Makasar/Indonesian words were adopted into the

Spear fishing is not as easy as it looks Photo: Peter Solness

Cath and Deb mix with the local Yolngu Photos: Peter Solness

Yolngu vocabulary, including 'rupiah' as the term for money. The locals believe that Bawaka is the home of Bayini, the mischievous spirit of a Makasar woman who's been incorporated into Yolngu mythology. If you're lucky you may even find Makasar pottery washed up on the beach.

The southeast Asian connection doesn't end there. Bawaka consists of just two small shacks nestled in a lush green bay lined with beaches of the finest powdered sand set against a backdrop of coconut palms. It looks like it stepped straight out of a Thailand tourism brochure. You'll also quickly discover that it's home to the best-located public phone box in Australia, which the locals quaintly refer to as the 'ocean phone'.

Not only is it exquisitely beautiful, but the whole area around Bawaka is also a potent site of Yolngu ancestor

A balmy evening on the beach Photo: Peter Solness

On the idyllic tropical beach at Bawaka **Photo**: Peter Solness

stories and Creation myths. Across the dunes at Yalangbara is the site where the Djang'kawu Sisters came ashore. This important Yolngu story varies from clan to clan across the region, but it broadly narrates the journey of two sisters who travelled to Arnhem Land by canoe across the sea from Baralku, the island of the dead. After arriving at Yalangbara, they journeyed overland through Yolngu country, naming places, plants and animals and creating freshwater springs.

Luckily this heady mix of physical beauty and spiritual power doesn't go to anyone's head and visitors to Bawaka are welcome to participate in whatever's going on. It's likely that you'll be invited to learn the rudimentaries of spear-fishing, which looks deceptively simple but isn't. You're more likely to end up stabbing yourself in the foot than catching a seafood dinner. Other possible maritime treats include mud-crabbing, collecting oysters, and turtle-, whale- and dolphin-spotting. There's also the prospect of bushwalking and getting involved in dances. If you're a woman you might even be invited for a bush sauna.

Visitors looking for nothing but a bit of sun and sand should note that Bawaka's picture-book waters may look enticing but they're also home to a four-metre saltwater crocodile, so swimming is not advised. The locals and the reptile have come to an understanding of sorts and in exchange for do-nations of food, the croc seems content to leave them well alone when they venture into the water. It has to be said though that the Yolngu version of 'swimming' is not much more than a quick dip in the shallows, usually with some-one acting as lookout. Visitors should treat the resident reptile with respect. Its presence is a simple fact of life at Bawaka – and no doubt yours will be too.

A seaside sprint **Photo:** Peter Solness

Now *this* is paradise **Photos:** Peter Solness

Tracks in superfine sand **Photo:** Peter Solness

WHERE

Set on the shores of Port Bradshaw, Bawaka is in the Northern Territory, on the east coast of the Gove Peninsula in northeastern Arnhem Land. It's a ninety-minute drive southeast of Nhulunbuy and an hour's drive southeast of Yirrkala; the last half-hour is along the beach.

WHEN

It's preferable to visit in the Dry (May to September), when sea breezes keep the temperature pleasant.

HOW

Yirrkala resident Timmy Burarrwanga runs Bawaka Cultural Tours (0437 387 135). He's the chairperson of the Yirrkala Dhanbul Community Association and Bawaka is his mother's homeland. Visitors to Bawaka can camp on the beach under a bough shelter, but visits must be arranged with Timmy in advance. You'll need some conservative beach clothes and a permit from the Northern Land Council (www.nlc.org.au/html/permits.html) in Nhulunbuy.

137

A writhing Rainbow Serpent rock painting at Ubirr, Kakadu National Park Photo: Richard I'Anson

Land of the Lightning Dreaming: Kakadu National Park

East of Darwin, the mesmerising sameness of the Top End's savannah woodland segues into a vast mosaic of wetlands and monsoonal rainforest rich in Aboriginal culture and wildlife. This is the world-famous Kakadu National Park, bounded to the east by the Arnhem Land escarpment and dissected by rivers that during cataclysmic wet-season storms burst their banks and inundate the surrounding plains. Tourists flock here to see wildlife spectacles, such as giant estuarine crocodiles and huge flocks of water birds, but superimposed on the rich natural tapestry is an ancient history of indigenous culture and one of the most accessible repositories of rock art in all of Australia.

In 1845 Ludwig Leichhardt was the first white explorer to visit the area, but it had already been continuously inhabited for at least 20,000 years – and perhaps longer – by the Bininj people. Aboriginal people helped Leichhardt's beleaguered expedition to cross the region's croc-infested wetlands, but poor old Ludwig eventually vanished in the Western Deserts, never to be seen again.

Some 500 Gagadju (also spelt Gagadu or Kakadu), Gundjehmi and Jawoyn people – the three major groups of traditional owners – continue to live in the park today, along with smaller clans such as the Mirrar. When the national park was declared in 1979, 'Kakadu' was chosen as the name that evoked the region's people and sense of place, and in 1984 Kakadu National Park received a rare dual World Heritage listing for both its natural and cultural importance. Aboriginal people play an active role in the running of Kakadu, and the land and wildlife are still managed with traditional fire regimes, as they have been for thousands of years under indigenous stewardship.

Above, from left: A blue-faced honeyeater sips nectar from a scarlet blossom **Photo:** Mitch Reardon; Red water lilies carpet Kakadu wetlands **Photo:** David Curl; Testament to a distant past: a Tasmanian tiger depicted in Aboriginal rock art **Photo:** Tom Boyden; Magpie geese wade through the shallows **Photo:** Martin Cohen

So intertwined are the natural and human histories of Kakadu that an understanding of one is impossible without an appreciation of the other. Bowali visitors centre, near Jabiru township, presents *gukburlerri* (indigenous) and *guhbele* (nonindigenous) interpretations of the region's culture, geology, wildlife and seasonal changes with state-of-the-art walk-through displays.

Warradjan Aboriginal Cultural Centre, fifty kilometres south at Cooinda, is housed in a circular building, designed to represent a meeting of peoples and also the *warradjan* (pig-nosed turtle). The Warradjan centre celebrates Aboriginality and delves deep into Bininj lore and traditions, introducing visitors to the moiety (skin classification) system and skin names. Both centres make excellent introductions to the park – escape the midday heat in one or other before an afternoon tour or a visit to a rock-art gallery.

There are about 5000 rock-art sites around the park, ranging in age from twenty thousand years to a few decades. Some are concentrated in large galleries that are readily accessible to the public, while others are out of bounds to visitors because they are private, sacred or inhabited by malevolent beings who must not be disturbed by those unfamiliar with the region's indigenous customs. North of the Arnhem Highway, Ubirr is a centuries-old Bininj gallery on a sandstone outcrop. Among the classic X-ray motifs of important food animals, such as fish, long-necked tortoises and goannas, are images of European ships, long-extinct thylacines (Tasmanian tigers) and giant kangaroos. Of major interest is the Rainbow Serpent painting, a women's business site that cannot be visited by Aboriginal men. In Kakadu the serpent is a woman, Kuriyali, who painted her image on the rock wall while on a journey through this area. According to the park's traditional owners, she is the most powerful spirit. If

139

Swimmers beware: the menacing profile of a saltwater crocodile breaks the surface at Yellow Water **Photo: John Banagan**

A rosy Ubirr flood plain at sunset, Kakadu National Park **Photo: Tom Boyden**

disturbed, Kuriyali can be very destructive, causing floods and earthquakes. After taking in the rock art, climb up the modest slope to Nardab Lookout and let Kakadu's magic seep in as the sun sets over the East Alligator floodplain to a symphony of cockatoos, barking owls and howling dingoes.

A turn-off south of Jabiru takes you to Nourlangie, a gigantic, red-sandstone monolith that is a living museum of Kakadu's best-known rock art. The name is a corruption of *nawulandja*, a word referring to an area bigger than the rock itself, and Nourlangie is a cultural and ecological micro-cosm of the Arnhem Land 'stone country' – land of the Lightning Dreaming. The rock's 200-metre-high bluffs have been eroded into countless overhangs and gullies that for millennia have provided shelter and livelihood for Aborigi-nal people. Nourlangie is renowned for galleries showing images of Namarrgon (Lightning Man), who is responsible

for all the spectacular electrical storms that occur in the Wet. A short self-guided walk leads to the main gallery, Anbangbang rock shelter, used by the Bininj people for 20,000 years to escape heat, rain and violent wet-season storms. Circular marks on rocks under the overhang show where they ground seeds for food and ochre for paint. In the 1960s a respected Aboriginal artist repainted this gallery. Gunwarddehwarde Lookout is reached via a series of open-air galleries and provides a panorama of the Arnhem Land escarpment or, if you're fit and adventurous there's the twelve-kilometre Barrk walk over the top of Nourlangie. On the way back to the Arnhem Highway, stop in at the superb but little-visited Nanguluwur Gallery, a long overhanging cliff displaying 30,000 years of Aboriginal rock art.

Kakadu offers dozens of other scenic attractions that change dramatically with the seasons and subtly from day

Electrifying image of Namarrgon (Lightning Man), Nourlangie Rock **Photo:** John Banagan

to day. Water birds, crocodiles and tourists congregate at ever-diminishing water holes during the Dry, when a dawn cruise on Yellow Water Billabong at Cooinda offers a wildlife spectacle unmatched anywhere in Australia. After the Wet you can witness the thundering spectacle of Jim Jim Falls (Barrhmarlam) and Twin Falls (Gungurdurl) in full spate, swollen with monsoonal rains, while in the south of the park you can climb the Arnhem Land escarpment then take a re-freshing dip at the foot of a waterfall in the famous Gunlom plunge pool. And a privileged few manage to visit Koolpin Gorge (Jarrangbarnmi), a restricted site that is taboo to the Jawoyn. In the early twentieth century mineral prospectors wanted to open the area up, but to the Jawoyn this was 'sickness country', and elders said if white man entered the area earthquakes and destruction would surely follow. Strangely enough, these hills are replete with uranium and, long before anyone had thought of nuclear weapons, the Jawoyn had divined the potential hazards of the area. Think about this as you watch *garnamarr*, Kakadu's ubiquitous red-tailed black-cockatoos winging lazily over woolly butts (a type of eucalyptus) with their 'creaking gate' call. The Jawoyn believe these huge black cockatoos always fly north, away from sickness country, where their tails caught fire…

Jim Jim Falls in full spate during the Wet
Photo: David Curl

WHERE

The northern entry station of Kakadu National Park is about 160 kilometres east of Darwin, in the Northen Territory. Access to the southern part of the park is through Pine Creek, 235 kilometres southeast of Darwin. Jabiru is the major service centre for Kakadu.

WHEN

The Dry (June to Septem-ber) is the most popular time to visit, but Kakadu really turns on the magic during the 'build-up' (Octo-ber to December) and the onset of the Wet. During the Wet access roads to Jim Jim and Twin Falls are closed and attractions in the south-ern part of the park, such as Gunlom, are only accessible by four-wheel drive.

HOW

Both Ubirr and Nourlangie have interpretive displays and well-marked trails, and rangers run free tours from June to September.

Guluyambi Cruise (1800 089 113) runs cruises guided by Aborigines, em-phasising indigenous culture and relationship with the land, on the East Alligator River year-round (check for Wet departure details). Look out for fresh- and saltwater crocodiles sunning them-selves on the banks.

Animal Tracks (08-8979 0145) offers a range of authentic hands-on experi-ences, including hunting and gathering and preparing bush foods and medicines; traditional fibre craft and bush-shelter construction; language instruction and stories about Aboriginal law, the Dreaming and Creation.

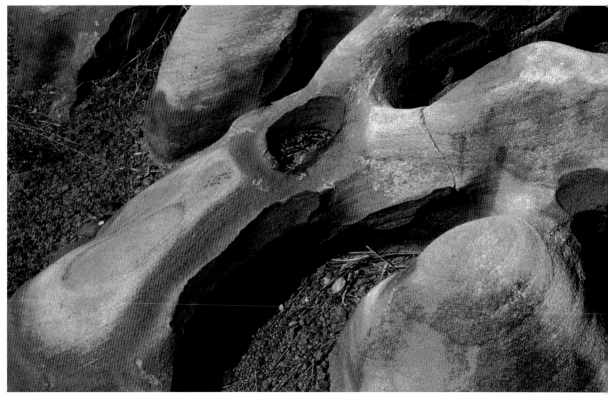

Bizarre rock formations on the Matilda Highway near Normanton, Queensland. **Photo:** Sally Dillon

Rainbow Serpent Country: Gulf Track

Steeped in history and lined by unmarked graves, the 1000-kilometre Gulf Track from Roper Bar in the Northern Territory's Top End to Normanton (p67) in northwestern Queensland crosses some of tropical Australia's wildest and most remote country. Until recent times the track was little more than a set of wheel ruts winding through the endless bush. Those days are gone, but there is still a powerful sense of adventure, thanks to the Gulf's vast untouched forests, the low population and lack of facilities, and the crocodiles that lurk in its numerous rivers.

Roper Bar, on the magnificent Roper River, is a popular fishing spot renowned for its barramundi and saratoga. The river here is over one hundred metres wide and lined by huge paperbark trees at the rock bar, which makes the river shallow. Steamships and large sailing vessels used to tie up at the bar to discharge cargo. The road to Ngukurr,

an Aboriginal community thirty kilometres east, crosses the river here, but to visit you need a permit from the Northern Land Council.

To the Waanyi people, who have enjoyed this spot for perhaps 30,000 years, Boodjamulla (Lawn Hill) National Park is Rainbow Serpent country. The idyllic water holes here were created during the Dreaming travels of Boodjamulla (the Rainbow Serpent) to provide permanent water to keep his skin wet. It is said that if Boodjamulla ever leaves the area, the water holes will dry up. The Rainbow Dreaming rock shelter in the gorge has an ochre painting thought to represent Boodjamulla, who is said to live in the Duwadarri water hole nearby. At the foot of the shelter are a grinding stone and a midden showing where Waanyi people have feasted on *malumalu*, the freshwater mussels once so abundant that they were known as 'water beef'. The

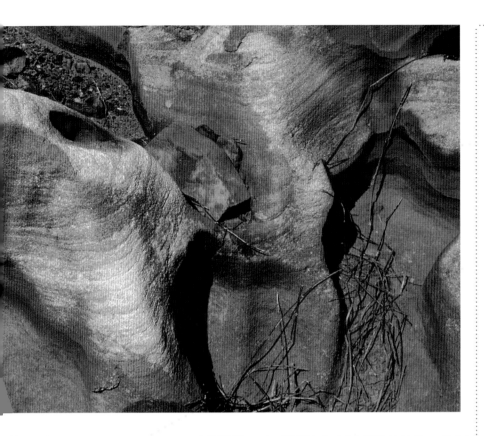

A freshwater crocodile floats in tranquil waters **Photo:** Chris Mellor

Wild Dog Dreaming shelter was formed during the Dreaming wanderings of the Ancestral Dingo, who on his journey from the south followed the Constance Range to the site, then journeyed further north to Doomadgee. The yellow ochre 'rainbow' shapes depicted at Wild Dog Dreaming are thought to represent arch-shaped objects held by performers during the wild dog or dingo dance. There are also many engravings, thought to be of great age, the most obvious of which are 'cup and ring' motifs.

The Riversleigh section of Boodjamulla is the World Heritage Area of the Australian Fossil Mammal Sites, one of the most significant fossil deposits in the world and the richest known fossil mammal deposit in Australia. Gondwanan life forms, which existed prior to the break up of this ancient continent, have been found here.

Paperbark and pandanus fringe the Roper River **Photo:** Richard l'Anson

WHERE
The Gulf Track runs for 1000 kilometres through the Northern Territory and Queensland, along the Gulf of Carpentaria.

WHEN
Travel is not recommended between December and April as it is extremely hot and humid, and heavy rain often closes the road for lengthy periods. In the build-up to the Wet (September onwards), temperatures can hit the forties.

HOW
Complacency and excessive speed are the track's major motoring hazards. You don't need a four-wheel drive in the Dry unless you take the tracks that lead to the coast; however, conventional vehicles need good ground clearance and solid suspension. The river crossings are usually no problem by June, when water levels drop to no more than 600 millimetres over the track.

For most of its length, the Gulf Track runs through Aboriginal land, cattle stations and national parks, and landowners will not be pleased to find you driving on their land without permission. Access to bush camping at river crossings is usually unrestricted. The Northern Land Council (www.nlc.org.au/html/permits.html) supplies permits.

Oz Tours Safaris (07-4055 9535) in Cairns has a nine-day Gulf Savannah tour that includes Boodjamulla National Park and the Riversleigh fossil site. Savannah Aviation (07-4745 5177) organises fishing trips from Burketown.

Just being out of the fast lane of city living natural landscape had a really calming effect

Some of the Torres Strait Islands are surrounded by stunning coral reefs Photo: Oliver Strewe

Crocodiles & Pearls: Torres Strait Islands

The Torres Strait Islands run like stepping stones from the top of Cape York to the south coast of Papua New Guinea, about 150 kilometres north of the Australian mainland. The Islanders came from Melanesia and Polynesia about 2000 years ago and are a unique and culturally distinct group of people who have absorbed and transformed influences from their neighbours, the Cape York Aborigines in the south and Papuans in the north. A melodious creole, showing traces of Papuan and mainland Aboriginal languages, is widely spoken in the Torres Strait.

Thursday Island (Waiben or TI, as the locals call it) is a multicultural hub with a laid-back charm and a stunningly beautiful outlook onto the surrounding islands. You can see the tip of Cape York from here and it's incredible to think of Australia's vast mainland stretching endlessly to the south. There are pearls, estuarine crocodiles and plenty

of hardy locals making their living in and on these waters. Islanders play by the water, as is obvious by the number of water activities people enjoy, but they also live by it. The sea forms much of their history, their living, their spirituality, all rolled into the strong waves of their independent cultures.

Tradition remains strong here. Formerly, the most powerful religious cult in the region was the Malo-Bomai cult, based on the heroic beings Malo and Bomai; it has been suggested that aspects of the cult still survive in Torres Strait Island Christianity. Islanders conduct a unique ceremony known as a 'tombstone opening', which marks the end of a period of mourning. A tombstone is unveiled and after a religious service there is a celebration with dancing and feasting. Many mainland Torres Strait Islanders return to the islands for these ceremonies.

and looking over that awe-inspiring
on me. — Cath

Above, from left: Extravagant headwear of the Mer (Murray) Islanders; Fried sardines on a stick from Ugar (Stephen Island); Fragrant frangipani (plumeria) headdress
Photos: Oliver Strewe

The pearling, trochus and trepang (sea cucumber) industries have shaped the recent history of this region. The Torres Strait pearling boom began in 1869 and in 1877 the administrative centre of the area was moved to Thursday Island from Somerset, on the tip of Cape York. By the 1890s the industry was dominated by Japanese pearlers, but TI had become a multicultural mix of indigenous people, white administrators and missionaries, pearlers and trepang fishermen from Japan, China, Malaya, the Philippines, Sri Lanka and the Pacific Islands. The island was evacuated during World War II and became the headquarters for the forces stationed in the strait. Today much of the wealth of the area still comes from the sea, particularly from the prawn and tropical-rock-lobster fisheries. Tourism is also playing a growing part.

Visitors often find exploring World War II relics and the War Museum at the Gateway Resort on Horn Island (Ngurapai) a highlight. This is the traditional land of the Kaurareg people, the northernmost group of the Aboriginal population, who were forcibly removed from their traditional country in the early 1920s. During World War II, Horn Island became a battle zone, suffering eight Japanese air raids. Among the 5000 troops stationed on the island was the 830-strong Torres Strait Light Infantry Battalion (TSLIB). Almost every able-bodied Islander man in the Torres Strait – over 700 volunteers – joined the TSLIB, with only about ten men staying behind to protect their families. This army tradition is still strong in the Torres and many young Islanders are in the Army Reserves.

Beyond TI and Horn Island, the other Torres Strait Islands exhibit a surprising variety. There are three main types. This rocky, mountaintop extension of the Great Dividing Range, making up most of the inner and western island groups,

Traditional dancer from Thursday Island wearing decorative foliage and a dhari headdress **Photo:** Trevor Creighton

Thursday Island, 'capital' of the Torres Strait Islands **Photo:** Oliver Strewe

includes Dauan (at the northernmost tip of the range); Thursday Island; Muralag (Prince of Wales Island) and Keriri (Hammond Island); Badu and Moa (St Pauls Island); as well as Boigu and Saibai Islands, which border Papua New Guinea. The central group of islands that extend to the east from TI are little more than coral cays: these are Iama (Yam Island), Warraber (Sue Island), Poruma (Coconut Island) and Masig (Yorke Island). The third type of islands are volcanic in origin and rise in the far east of the strait, at the very northern end of the Great Barrier Reef. These are Mer (Murray Island), home of Eddie Mabo; Erub (Darnley Island) and Ugar (Stephen Island) – some of the most spectacular and picturesque in the area.

While Thursday Island is the 'capital' of Torres Strait, there are seventeen inhabited islands in all. TI is little more than four-and-a-half square kilometres in area, with the main

town of Port Kennedy on its southern shore. The population is around 3000. Outside of Thursday and Horn Islands, the largest group of people are found on Boigu, where the population numbers around 400. Most of the islands welcome visitors and have some form of accommodation to offer. There's a resort on Poruma, Masig also has a small tourist facility, and another tourist/conference facility is underway on Warraber.

Mer, a fertile island in the eastern group, became famous when Eddie 'Koiki' Mabo and three other Murray Islanders commenced legal action to have traditional title to their land recognised in Australian common law. After ten years of hearings, the High Court of Australia found in 1992 that the Mer people owned the land prior to annexation. This simple decision put paid to the fiction of *terra nullius* (land owned by nobody), which had underpinned the European

146

WHERE
The Torres Strait Islands have been a part of Queensland since 1879; they lie between the tip of Cape York and Papua New Guinea.

WHEN
Each year on 1 July, the Coming of the Light festival is celebrated throughout the islands to commemorate the day in 1871 when the London Missionary Society landed on Erub, bringing Christianity to the Torres Strait. Other events include the Torres Strait Cultural Festival, held around July on even-numbered years and featuring sporting events, cultural performances and craft and food stalls; and the Torres Strait Music Festival in September.

HOW
The Torres Strait Regional Authority site (www.tsra.gov.au) includes information on each populated island. For information on visiting the island communities, availability of permits, and accommodation, contact individual island councils directly.

The airport for the inner islands is on Horn Island, a fifteen-minute ferry trip from Thursday Island. On TI, the helpful Peddells Ferry & Tour Bus Service (07-4069 1551) offers boat and bus tours as well as general information. Also check out Rebel Marine (07-40691586) at Rebel Wharf.

Most of the inhabited islands have an airstrip and a number of airlines operate light aircraft in the strait.

occupation of Australia, and paved the way for the 1993 Commonwealth Native Title Act. Tragically, Koiki died only months before the judgement was handed down.

Islanders are usually very hospitable and proud of their culture. You could well find yourself learning how to weave a basket or be invited along on a dinghy trip. In some cases the relevant island council can help to arrange these sorts of activities for you. Local pearls, original artworks and intricately carved spears and drums are available at selected shops on TI.

Very few people make the effort to see this gorgeous part of the world, but the chance to catch a glimpse of life in an isolated island community is exactly what makes the islands so appealing. The other main attractions are fishing (for good eaters or for big, bad game), the coral (which makes for beautiful snorkelling) and the beaches.

Maisie Mari, from Warraber (Sue Island), making damper **Photo:** Oliver Strewe

A triple-carriage road train thunders up the Cape York Peninsula **Photo:** Oliver Strewe

Right to the Tip:
Cape York

Cape York Peninsula is one of the last great frontiers of Australia, and it's not for the faint-hearted. It's a vast patchwork of tropical savannah cut through by numerous majestic rivers and streams, while along its eastern flank lies the northern section of the Great Dividing Range. Among these ragged peaks and deep valleys are some of the best and most significant rainforests in Australia. Streams tumble down the rocky mountains to the sea, where just offshore the coral ramparts of the Great Barrier Reef stretch over thousands of kilometres. The reef is protected as part of a marine park, and much of the land mass of the peninsula is protected in a number of spectacular but rarely visited national parks. Known simply as 'the Tip', the area bordering the Torres Strait is the goal of most travellers in Cape York (traditionally known as Pajinka), lured by the chance to stand on the northernmost tip of mainland Australia.

Vast areas of Cape York Peninsula are designated Aboriginal land, while the rest is mainly taken up with large pastoral holdings and national parks. Covering an area of around 207,000 square kilometres, about the same size as the state of Victoria, the peninsula has a population of only 18,000 people. Most live in remote Cooktown (p156), on the southeastern coast; in the 'lawn-world' of mining town Weipa, where lawns are an obsession and sprinklers ubiquitous; and in a handful of other small townships.

Traditionally, the Cape's indigenous inhabitants lived a seminomadic lifestyle, relying heavily on the sea and their double-outrigger canoes. They were great warriors and there's a long history of tensions with the European invaders, as well as between local tribal groups. Before the arrival of Europeans a large number of different Aboriginal tribal groups were spread throughout the Cape, while a

Fishing for turtles in the clear tropical waters of Cape York Photo: Oliver Strewe

WHERE
Cape York is the northern-most tip of mainland Australia, in Far North Queensland.

WHEN
Like other areas this far north, the Wet greatly restricts vehicle movement on Cape York Peninsula. The best time to go is as early in the Dry as possible (June) when the country-side is greener, there is more water around, there are fewer travellers and the roads are generally better. The peak period is between July and August, with the last vehicles leaving the Cape by the end of October.

Several local festivals are held in the Cape through-out the year. Bamaga Annual Show takes place in August or September and features rodeo events, horse races, carnival stalls and an amusement fair. The Croc Eisteddfod is a cross-cultural festival held at the Weipa North State School around mid-July and draw-ing together communities from around the Cape.

HOW
Four-wheel drive is the only way to travel the Cape. A well-constructed off-road trailer can be taken all the way to the top, but other trailers will fall apart along the way. Caravans can make it to Cooktown via the inland route, or as far as Weipa if driven with care. You need to carry all the usual gear for travelling in a remote area so that you are as self-sufficient as possible, and you must carry water.

(continued on p151)

unique group of people inhabited the is-lands dotted across the reef-strewn Torres Strait (p144). These Torres Strait Islanders influenced Aboriginal tribal groups near the top of the peninsula and vice versa. Their rich multicultural heritage is alive today and travellers will see much of it on their way to the top.

At the start of the twentieth century, Aboriginal people from the various com-munities in the region established and ran their own settlement at Injinoo (Cowal Creek), which was not officially recorded by the Australian government until 1916. The community managed its own affairs until World War II brought an influx of

Meandering river south of Weipa Photo: Oliver Strewe

Kicking up the bulldust during a cattle muster **Photo:** Oliver Strewe

thousands of soldiers to the area and the Department of Native Affairs took over the area's administration. The Injinoo community council has identified five major groups living in the community today, and together their traditional lands are known as the Northern Peninsula Area (NPA). In the late 1940s Torres Strait Islanders from Saibai Island established the townships of Bamaga and Seisia a few kilometres from Injinoo. In 1963 Aboriginal people from Marpuna (Mapoon), north of Weipa, were forcibly removed to New Mapoon to make way for mining, while people from the Lockhart River set up the township of Umagico. Bamaga became the administrative centre of the region; it's now home to the largest Torres Strait Islander community and makes a perfect stopover before the last stretch to the Tip. With this background in mind, you could consider your journey through the Cape as a journey across nations.

The trip from Cairns to the top of Cape York Peninsula is about a thousand kilometres via the shortest route. Initially, the corrugated road you follow is known officially as the Peninsula Developmental Road, but once that heads away to Weipa you can follow the historic and adventurous Overland Telegraph Track, with its numerous challenging creek crossings. You can avoid the creeks by taking the new but longer bypasses, and instead, shake, rattle and roll along these badly corrugated roads. Crossing the creeks is shorter and more fun, but team up with someone with a winch just in case you get bogged. Even in the Dry most major creek crossings have water in them; however, it's not the water that's the main problem but the steep banks on either side. Take care and read the small print on your insurance policy.

The section of road from the Moreton Telegraph Station to the Jardine River Ferry is the best part of the trip, with

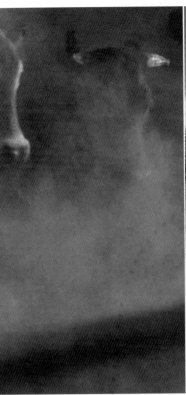

Fording the Mitchell River near Mount Mulgrave **Photo:** Oliver Strewe

Permits are not required for travelling to Cape York via the main routes described.

However, you do need a permit to camp on Aboriginal land, which is nearly all the land north of the Dulhunty River. Most people pay when they get to the Jardine River crossing; you can also get a permit from the Injinoo Community Council (07-4069 3252).

Countless tour operators run trips to the Cape. Try the following companies: Exploring Oz Safaris (07-4093 8347, 1300 888 112), Heritage 4WD Tours (07-4038 2628) and Oz Tours Safaris (07-4055 9535, 1800 079 006).

some great creek crossings and excellent camp sites. Take your time and enjoy all the delights the Cape has to offer. It's 180 kilometres but following the rough track along the Overland Telegraph Track means the trip will take at least a very long day, even if all goes well. Among the scattered timber and blanket of grass you can see cycad palms, in places forming dense stands.

The eastern side of the NPA is dominated by the Jardine River National Park, on the traditional lands of the Anaggamuthi, Atambaya, Yadhaykenu, Gudang and Wathatni peoples. There are many sites of spiritual significance here. The park is jointly managed by its traditional owners and you can camp at some magical sites within the park, such as Eliot Falls or Captain Billy Landing. Indian Head Falls drops into a small, sheer-sided ravine, and Fruit Bat Falls is a beautiful spot for a picnic or swim. Along the banks of the creeks around here you will find fascinating pitcher plants: these carnivorous plants trap insects in the liquid at the bottom of a 'pitcher', where their nutrients are absorbed by the plant. It is a unique adaptation to living in rocky areas that are poor in nutrients.

Remember, the Jardine River is inhabited by estuarine crocodiles and, although you might not be able to see them, they are definitely there. In December 1993 a man was killed by a crocodile while he was swimming to the ferry at the ferry crossing.

Below, from top: Native kapok has edible flowers; Fruit of the forest
Photos: Oliver Strewe

152

Cath & Deb's Bush Travel Tips

THINGS TO PACK

CATH

Running shoes: My running shoes go everywhere with me as I walk or run every day. They represent a form of solitude and therapy for me. My favourite run was the one I took on a dirt track going to Katherine, the colour of the land and the light were just splendid. One morning in Arnhem Land I came face to face with a huge water buffalo. We both froze, but he was the one who ran away – ten times my size and he was more scared than I was!

Bathing gloves: They help you have a 'bush bath' without using much water. You wet the gloves and put soap on them and you can wash yourself like that, and only use water to rinse yourself. It's been a really useful trick!

Toothbrush: An absolute necessity. I don't enjoy starting the day without clean teeth, especially when you are travelling in the bush and there is dust absolutely everywhere.

Water: I always drink loads of water. It's important for your mental awareness and your strength, especially when you are travelling.

DEB

Music: I have a little bit of everything, from country to dance. On this trip, we listened to Pigram Brothers (from Broome), Fitzroy Xpress (from the Kimberley) and Charley Pride. Country seemed to fit the journey. You can't travel down a dust track without country music blaring.

Sweets: I'm a lolly addict. I had to have my lolly bag at all times. It's a great sugar fix, to keep your energy up along those looooong journeys.

Walking shoes: You can't be in the bush without a good pair of boots. My favourites are a pair of Blundstones or the cowboy boots I bought in Halls Creek. Apart from being practical you also look pretty cool!

Hat: I also love my cowbie hat I bought in Halls Creek. I wear it all the time even on the weekend in Melbourne. It's dented and covered in red dust, it's a great look!

Camera: I love taking pictures, I take pictures of everything and I came back with a load of great scenery pics.

BUSH FOOD

CATH

Bush damper: My favourite bush food was the cycad nut we ate in Marparu. They grind and soak the nuts for five days and mush them together into a flour, it's the most amazing bread I have ever eaten.

DEB

Fish: Catching the food yourself and throwing it on the hot stones.

CAMPING

CATH

Swags (canvas bed roll with mattress): I think the swag is an excellent invention. I'm happy in my swag because it's functional, it keeps me warm and dry, it's tough and it's durable. I sound like I'm selling them!

DEB

Tents: Pick one that doesn't have too many bits to it because it can be tricky to put them up at night: the simpler the better.

Swags: My mission was by the end of the trip to be able to roll a really good swag. It's got to be pretty tight. You can't go bush without a good swag.

DRIVING

CATH

Long drives: Deb's mucking around kept me amused. Other times we'd have deep serious discussions. When Deb slept I'd keep to my own thoughts, it's quite relaxing because you don't have to negotiate a lot of turns on those straight roads.

Tyres: I have learnt how to change a tyre. When you drive in the bush you definitely need to pack more than one spare tyre. We blew five of them!

DEB

Long drives: The best way to resist boredom on the long drives is to put on music full blast.

Tyres: I still don't know how to change them. My tip is, if you don't know how to do it, make sure you travel with someone who does!

An all-ages show: the Laura Aboriginal Dance Festival **Photo:** Paul Dymond

Quixotic Quinkans: Laura

Imagine coming upon a rock face covered in paintings that are part Hieronymus Bosch and part Pablo Picasso. You see an evil frog-like spirit with knobbly knees, elbows and a large penis, an emu on its side, a turtle and other paintings in yellow, mauve and orange. This is the first of the Split Rock Galleries of Quinkan art, one of more than 1200 galleries discovered in the escarpment country south of the town of Laura in Far North Queensland. Rated as one of the greatest art styles of Aboriginal Australia, Quinkan art gets its name from the human-style spirit figures with unusually shaped heads, called Quinkans, which appear frequently in this region. The tall skinny ones are said to be 'good' spirits, while the squat ones with knobbly knees, arms and other bits are 'bad'.

These stunning galleries contain fine paintings of kangaroos, dingoes, wallabies, emus, brush turkeys, crocodiles,

turtles, fish, snakes and flying foxes – in fact, all the wildlife and bush tucker that can still be seen along the rivers and plains today. Spiritual figures, guardians and ancestral beings also point to a lifestyle that was rich in culture and religious beliefs. Numerous paintings of naked male and female human figures could be connected to fertility or love magic, while the upside-down figures might be attempts at sorcery. Other figures seem to be dancing. While the rock art is difficult to date, it is known that Aboriginal people have been living in the area for at least 33,000 years. Much mystery still surrounds this art as the Quinkan artists were killed by settlers or disease in the 1873–83 Palmer River gold rush.

It is a hot, steep, twenty-minute climb to the three Split Rock Galleries, so you might as well carry on and walk along the top of the escarpment and enjoy the panoramic

Giant Horse Gallery, near Laura **Photo:** Oliver Strewe

WHERE
Laura is 317 kilometres
north of Cairns on the Peninsula Development Road
to the tip of Cape York.

WHEN
The best time to visit is in
the cooler winter months
(June to August). Try to
make it here in June of
an odd-numbered year to
see the Laura Aboriginal
Dance Festival. Bring-
ing together Aboriginal
communities from all over
Cape York, this three-day
event features dancing,
music, crafts and other activities such as spear- and
boomerang-throwing.

HOW
The Quinkan Regional
Cultural Centre (07-4060
3457) in Laura can organ-
ise tours of the Split Rock
Galleries and other nearby
sites, including Mushroom
Rock and Giant Horse, with
Aboriginal guides; if given
advance notice they can
also do trips to White Ibis,
one of the Quinkan sites,
with two Aboriginal Elders.

A highlight of the Cape
York tours run by Wilder-
ness Challenge (07-4035
4488) is a visit to the Split
Rock Galleries. Billy Tea
Bush Safaris (07-4032
0077) also offers Cape
York tours that include
Quinkan country and visits
to rock-art sites.

views from the Turtle Lookout. Next, have a look round the
Guguyalangi Galleries – a group of galleries with more than
a dozen overhangs adorned with a vast array of figures,
animals and implements.

It's also well worth a visit to the Ang-Gnarra Visitor Centre in
Laura, which has books and information on the Quinkans.
There's a caravan park, pool and playground here, and a
bush-tucker trail out the back with signs explaining some of
the local bush foods.

A dusty thirty-six kilometres west of the Peninsula Development Road, Jowalbinna Bush Camp was established by
Steve Trezise, whose father Percy was the first white man to
see and catalogue many of the Quinkan sites in the 1950s.
You can stay here and join one of the many excellent guided
walks to the art and ceremonial sites in the area.

Shaking it at Laura Aboriginal Dance
Festival **Photo:** Paul Dymond

Young women from Koah dancing at the Laura Aboriginal Dance Festival **Photo:** Paul Dymond

First Contact:
Cooktown

Cooktown is just far enough away from Cairns, and just difficult enough to reach, to have remained relatively untouched by mass tourism. It has the seedy, laid-back charm of a frontier town and draws in visitors on the trail of its fascinating past. The 'Queen of the North', as the town is often called, may be relatively quiet these days, but it's had two moments of prominence that make it no stranger to the history books.

On 17 June 1770 Cooktown became the site of Australia's first nonindigenous settlement when Captain James Cook beached his barque, the *Endeavour*, on the banks of its river and stayed for forty-eight days to make repairs.

While Cook had amicable contacts with local Guugu-Yimidhirr people, race relations turned sour a century later when Cooktown was founded and became the unruly port for

the 1873–83 Palmer River gold rush, which took place 140 kilometres southwest. Hell's Gate, a narrow pass on the track between Cooktown and the Palmer River, was the scene of frequent ambushes as Guugu-Yimidhirr warriors tried to stop their lands being overrun. Battle Camp, about sixty kilometres inland from Cooktown, was the site of a major battle in 1873 between European settlers and Aborigines.

To find out more, visit the fascinating James Cook Historical Museum. There's a room devoted to Aboriginal artefacts and a hall covering the exploits of Captain Cook, including a panel describing the first white contact with the Guugu-Yimidhirr and reproductions of Sydney Parkinson's drawings from 1770 of indigenous people.

On the Cooktown foreshore, about a hundred metres past the statue of Captain James Cook, is the Milbi Wall (Story

WHERE
Cooktown is 332 kilo-
metres north of Cairns, in
Far North Queensland. The
last thirty kilometres of the
trip is on unsealed roads.

WHEN
The route may be closed
during the Wet (January
to March) – check with
Cooktown police (07-4069
5320) before heading off.

The best time to come is
for the Hopevale Show &
Rodeo, a rowdy four-day
affair staged in July or
August each year.

HOW
The Gungarde Aboriginal
Centre (07-4069 5412)
is south of the Cooktown
Hotel.

The James Cook Historical
Museum (07-4069 5386)
is closed in March.

Cooktown Tours (07-4069
5125) offers four-wheel-
drive trips to the Split
Rock Galleries (p154) near
Laura, and Lakefield Na-
tional Park (Queensland's
second-largest national
park), best known for its
wetlands and prolific bird
life. They also do trips to
Coloured Sands (an area
of spectacular sand dunes)
via the Hopevale Aboriginal
community.

Driving to the top of Cooktown Hill **Photo:** Jenny & Tony Enderby

Wall) built by the Gungarde Aboriginal community. It
depicts Guugu-Yimidhirr history, culture and stories in a
snaking, mosaic wall. The Gungarde Aboriginal Centre has a
small selection of work by local and Cape York Aboriginal
artists.

The Hopevale Aboriginal community, north of Cooktown,
was established in 1886 by a Lutheran missionary to aid
the decimated and dispossessed survivors of the Guugu-
Yimidhirr people in the wake of the Palmer River gold
rush.

Community-made artefacts, including firesticks (lighted
sticks carried from camp to camp by Aborigines to light
fires), stone axes, spears, boomerangs, didjeridus and art
are available at the Hopevale community Learning Centre
in town.

Kids from Hopevale at the
Laura Aboriginal Dance Festival
Photo: Paul Dymond

157

Tight-lipped white-lipped tree frogs in the Daintree **Photo:** Martin Cohen

Strangler Figs & Salties:
The Daintree & Cape Tribulation

Part of the UNESCO Wet Tropics World Heritage area, which stretches from Townsville to Cooktown, the region from the Daintree River north to Cape Tribulation is extraordinarily beautiful and one of the few places in the world where the tropical rainforest meets the sea. Within this area is Daintree National Park, which stretches inland from Mossman Gorge to the Bloomfield River and boasts thirty per cent of Australia's frog, marsupial and reptile species, sixty-five per cent of its bat and butterfly species and twenty per cent of its bird species.

There are several walks in Daintree National Park, but the circular track is perhaps the best. It passes under tall, shady, dripping rainforest trees and takes about an hour to walk. One unusual tree to look out for is the strangler fig, which starts life high on the branch of another tree and sends roots down towards the ground. Gradually the roots

join together around the trunk of the host tree, which is eventually strangled to death. Bird's-nest ferns, orchids and brilliant blue Ulysses butterflies are also features of the walk. Look closely and you might see a tree-climbing kangaroo or a rare Boyd forest dragon clinging to a branch and watching for insects to devour. You can swim in pools in the river, but take care as people have drowned here.

Daintree Village, outside the park, has a timber museum and craft shops. Beyond the village is the Daintree River Ferry. The river is a haven for the saltwater crocodile and there have been many fatal attacks here, so it is important not to step close to the riverbank. Swimming, obviously, is out of the question.

At the Daintree Discovery Centre there is an aerial walkway and a twenty-three-metre tower up to the rainforest canopy.

Marrdja Boardwalk, further on, is an excellent thirty-minute walk through rainforest and mangrove swamps. Put on insect repellent if you don't want to donate blood to various insect species, some of which are microscopic but voracious. Guided tours led by local Kuku-Yalanji people are a great way to get insight into the region's wildlife, bush tucker and medicine. You can see a traditional dwelling and a demonstration of paint-making, and enjoy tea and damper under bark shelter after the walk.

The coast road follows the broad Bloomfield River before crossing it thirty kilometres north of Cape Tribulation. Cape Tribulation is famous for the lush rainforest that tumbles down the hills to the high-tide marks on the white sandy beaches, usually almost deserted. The Wujal Wujal Aboriginal community is on the northern bank of the river. Students from Wujal Wujal have created and erected twenty-four signs along the route that give the Kuku-Yalanji names for landmarks, such as Kija (Roaring Meg) and Jukar (Bloomfield Beach).

For something a bit different, the Karnak Playhouse is a 500-seat open-air amphitheatre in Miallo, next to Daintree National Park. A regular attraction is the hi-tech Creation laser show, in which fibre optics and three-dimensional effects accompany a performance by the Karnak Bama Dance Troupe.

Above, from top: Emu apple fruit and coloured leaves decorate the rainforest floor Photo: Mitch Reardon; Fan-leaf palms and the rainforest canopy above Photo: Peter Ptschelinzew

WHERE
The Daintree–Cape Tribulation area is in Far North Queensland, ninety kilometres north of Cairns.

WHEN
The Dry, roughly May to October, offers warm days and cool nights with low humidity. The Wet, November to April, brings torrential rains and balmier temperatures. Note that the beaches are off-limits from October to May due to marine stingers (box jellyfish).

HOW
The road to Cape Tribulation is sealed and does not require a four-wheel drive.

Kuku-Yalanji Dreamtime Walks (07-4098 2595) runs two-hour walks in Mossman Gorge, a picturesque section of Daintree National Park, with traditional custodians.

Entry to Wujal Wujal is by permit only – contact the Wujal Wujal Aboriginal Council (07-4060 8155). You'll need to state your intended dates of travel, the reason for your visit, the number of people in your party and your proposed length of stay.

A local makes the most of flood water during a rain storm **Photo:** Paul Dymond

Capital of the North: Cairns Area

The unofficial capital of the far north, Cairns is one of Australia's top tourist destinations. In a lush tropical setting, the city has an irrepressible energy and is a fabulous base for exploring the surrounding areas. You'll meet a lot of indigenous folk in the centre of town, and there are a number of Aboriginal communities around Cairns. This diverse little town is also a favourite for the Torres Strait Islander community.

To get into the tropical atmosphere, go for a wander in the Flecker Botanic Gardens. The gardens lie under the shadow of Mount Whitfield and feature an Aboriginal plant–use garden full of the many rainforest plants used by the Djabuganjdiji, Gungganjdiji, Yidinjdiji and Yirrganjdiji peoples.

The Yarrabah Aboriginal community started as an Anglican mission in 1892, combining the local tribes who had been driven off their land by the wholesale clearance of forest for sugar cane and cattle. The name (originally Yarraburra) refers to the white-bellied sea eagle (also known as an osprey, or fish hawk), and its flight as it hunts.

Around Cairns are a couple of great cultural centres offering insights into local indigenous culture. Tjapukai Aboriginal Cultural Park northwest of Cairns features theatres, a museum, an art gallery and a traditional camp site. Tjapukai communities and Elders own the land and have a substantial share in the venture.

Rainforestation Nature Park, on the Kennedy Highway just east of the Kuranda turn-off, hosts the Pamagirri Dancers, who perform a selection of dances and songs illustrating Dreaming legends from various parts of north Queensland. There are two performances daily of eight dances, including

A diver bedazzled by colourful coral, Great Barrier Reef near Cairns **Photo:** Nigel Marsh

WHERE
Cairns is the tourism and business centre of Far North Queensland. It's at the end of the Bruce Highway and the railway line from Brisbane.

WHEN
Cairns is super-wet between January and March so unless you have monsoonal tendencies, save your visit for the dryer months (May to October). You don't need a permit to visit Yarrabah community.

HOW
Indigenous Organisations Cairns is a regional centre, and many organisations that operate in the Cape are headquartered here. Check out Rainforestation (07-4093 9033).

A pint-sized slice of paradise on the Great Barrier Reef near Cairns **Photo:** Peter Hendrie

the Mosquito Dance, the Silent Snake and the Cassowary Dance. Also included are demonstrations of boomerang- and spear-throwing and didjeridu-playing; a walk-through Aboriginal village; and a chance to talk to musicians, artists and weapon makers demonstrating their skills in the Pamagirri Cultural Centre.

If you prefer something more casual, the Kuranda Markets (for food and essentials such as emu oil) and Heritage Markets (for touristy arts and crafts) are always a lively experience.

Shiny fern leaves in the Flecker Botanic Gardens, Cairns
Photo: Richard l'Anson

A stormy sky hovers over pandanus trees in the wetlands near Townsville Photo: Lawrie Williams

From Outback to Tropics: Townsville Area

Meeting place of the outback and the tropics, Townsville borders three traditional areas: Nyawaygi country, Gugu-Badhun country and Bindul country. Its white history is black: in the 1870s local Aborigines were often kidnapped for work on pearling and fishing vessels. After 1918, many were forcibly moved to Palm Island, which became the focus of the area's Aboriginal community life for several decades.

After World War II Torres Strait Islanders began arriving in Townsville to work on the railway. They also formed the back-bone of the sugar-cane and pearling industries (as they did in Broome and Darwin). Still more came to town in the 1960s and today Townsville is a major site of Islander culture. Just look for the bright colours in Townsville's main streets.

While you're here, check out the fabulous Museum of Tropical Queensland. Its displays reflect the Townsville region's

rich Aboriginal culture and its more recent but strong associations with the Torres: some 400 artefacts and artworks have been collected here over the past 100 years. Behold the snakeskin lighter cover and the woven-grass fly swat! Other exhibits describe the life and times of native-title warrior Eddie 'Koiki' Mabo (p146), and the lives of Islander men and women during World War II.

The magnificent but troubled Palm Island group off the coast of Townsville consists of ten main islands. All are Aboriginal reserves, apart from Orpheus, which is mostly national park and heavily forested, and nearby Pelorus, which is still crown land. The Aboriginal names of the main islands are Goolboddi (Orpheus), Yanooa (Pelorus), Cul-garool (Brisk), Inoogoo (Curacao), Garoogubbee (Eclipse), Soopun (Esk), Carbooroo (Falcon), Eumilli (Fantome), Havannah and Bukaman (Great Palm).

Contemporary paintings on a wall in Castle Hill **Photo:** Ross Barnett

Townsville's city lights **Photo:** Ross Barnett

Ecotourism companies run camping and sailing trips to the islands. The only accommodation is at the Palm Island Motel on Palm Island and an exclusive resort on Orpheus, which lies about twenty kilometres off the coast east of Ingham. Orpheus is a continental island (the tip of an underwater mountain), which is about eleven kilometres long and less than one kilometre wide. Here you might see nesting turtles, as well as lots of bird life and some of the best fringing reef to be found on any of the Great Barrier Reef islands. It's a quiet, secluded island good for camping, snorkelling and diving. There are three national-park camping grounds and a giant-clam research station.

The oldest pub in town: the Criterion Hotel **Photo:** John Banagan

WHERE
North-coast Queensland is home to energetic Townsville and the Palm Islands, about twenty kilometres offshore. To get here, take the Bruce Highway all the way along the tropical coast. The Flinders Highway scoots west across to the Northern Territory from here and the Great Barrier Reef lies east, two hours away.

WHEN
Townsville's great from April to December; otherwise pack a breatheable rain jacket.

HOW
Unless you're part of an extended family from the Palm Island group, you have to get written permission from Palm Island Aboriginal Council (07-4770 1177), on Palm Island, or the Department of Aboriginal and Torres Strait Islander Policy office (07-4799 7470) before you can land there. You'll need to say when and why you want to come over, how many people will be with you, and how long you're planning to stay.

Lucinda Reef Island Charter Service (07-4777 8220) operating from Lucinda, and Orpheus Island Diving, Fishing & Transfer Services (0407 378 968) operating from Taylor's Beach, near Ingham, will transfer campers out to Orpheus (and to Pelorus, too).

Australian Eco Adventures offers tailored ecotours of the Townsville area (www.ozeco.com.au).

A humpback whale and her calf frolic in Whitsunday waters **Photo:** Bob Charlton

Coral Reefs & Forested Hills: Whitsunday Islands

Going bush isn't just about driving the dusty highways, stumbling across an oasis in the vast sandy desert and admiring monolith rocks. Just as well, too, or you could miss out on this beautiful region of Australia. White-sand beaches, turquoise water, coral reefs and densely forested interiors will greet you on the tranquil Whitsundays. You'll find all those classic island-style activities abound here: snorkelling, diving, whale-watching, fishing, sailing, and just lazing on the beach.

The seventy-four Whitsundays are mostly continental islands – the tips of underwater mountains – but many of them have fringing coral reefs. The Great Barrier Reef, however, is at least sixty kilometres away. The islands, mostly hilly and wooded, and the passages between them, are stunning to behold, and all but four of the islands are either predominantly or completely national park. The resort islands are Hayman, Hamilton, Daydream, Linderman, Brampton, Long, Hook and South Molle; most of the other islands are uninhabited.

Curiously, the Whitsundays are misnamed – Captain Cook didn't really sail through them on Whit Sunday. When he returned to England it was found that his meticulously kept log was a day out because he had not allowed for crossing the International Date Line!

The Ngaro Aboriginal people, who were the original inhabitants of the area, were accomplished mariners and travelled between the islands in three-part bark canoes that were capable of open-sea journeys. Middens, the remnants of quarries and fish traps are found on a number of islands, and there is an Aboriginal art site that you can visit at Nara Inlet on Hook Island.

Sea-worn pebbles and bone-dead coral Photo: Gareth McCormack

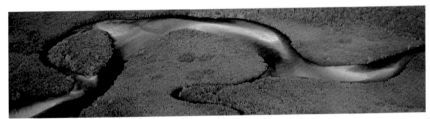

A river winds through mangroves. Photo: Peter Hendrie

The Coral Beach Track at Airley Beach on the mainland is a self-guiding one-kilometre track explaining the traditional uses of some of the region's rainforest and mangrove plants. It was created with the help of the Giru Dala Council of Elders, the traditional custodians of the Whitsunday homeland area. Leaflets are available at the trailhead.

Seaplanes float near a reef Photo: John Banagan

WHERE
The Whitsundays are 150 kilometres north of Mackay, in Queensland.

WHEN
The average maximum temperature in the summer months is thirty-one degrees Celsius, and the average high in winter is twenty-three degrees Celsius. Most tourist activity occurs between May and October, when southerners flee their colder winter. Stingers (box jellyfish) are out in force from October/November to April/May – get into a clingy stinger suit if you want to swim then. Humpback whales visit from July to September.

HOW
Boats of all kinds depart for the islands from Shute Harbour regularly. The nearest mainland airport is Proserpine. It's also possible to fly direct to Hamilton Island from Melbourne, Sydney, Brisbane and Cairns. By rail, the *Sunlander* will also get you there.

Wavelength Reef Charters (07-4099 5031) has advanced accreditation as a genuine ecotourism service and runs an Outer Barrier Reef snorkelling tour that includes a reef biology presentation by a qualified marine biologist. Barefoot Cruises (07-4946 1777) operates a range of three- and six-night cruises to the Whitsunday Islands and Great Barrier Reef on fully crewed sailing boats and luxury cruisers.

Mountains & Plains

Picking up tips at the two-up school just outside Kalgoorlie **Photo:** Andrew Marshall & Leanne Walker

A Cross-Eyed Killer:
Great Eastern Hwy

Stretching east from the outskirts of Perth all the way to Kalgoorlie-Boulder, the Great Eastern Highway runs through barren but beautiful countryside punctuated by unusual, often dramatic rock formations. The most famous landmark in this region is Wave Rock, a curl of sweeping rock fifteen metres high that seems on the point of breaking into foam, even if it is 200 kilometres from the nearest stretch of coast.

Nyoongar stories link the rock with the evil Milky Way woman, but there are even more interesting associations with nearby Mulka's Cave. This art site features dozens of faded hand stencils and several barely discernible paintings.

It's believed that the highest stencils were left by Mulka, who was the fruit of a forbidden liaison between a man and woman from the wrong skin groups. He was immensely

strong but had crossed eyes, which prevented him from becoming a good hunter. Mulka, who lived in the cave, turned to eating children, and when his mother chastised him he killed her as well. Forced to flee, he made it as far as Dumbleyung, 150 kilometres to the south, where he was caught and speared to death.

About 300 metres from Mulka's Cave is a *gnamma* (rock hole) that would have been a valuable source of drinking water for Nyoongar people – perhaps even for Mulka himself. Also in the area is Hippo's Yawn, a traditional birthing place.

The Great Eastern Highway leads you to Kalgoorlie-Boulder, and the chance to pick up a unique souvenir, or unroll your swag beneath a glittering display of stars on a cultural tour. The town was founded when long-time prospector Paddy

The terraces of the Sons of Gwalia mine near Kalgoorlie Photo: Peter Ptschelinzew

Hannan set out from Coolgardie in search of another gold strike, and proved that sometimes beggars can be choosers. Stumbling across the surface gold that sparked the 1893 gold rush, he inadvertently chose the site of Kalgoorlie for a township. When surface sparkles subsided, the miners dug deeper, extracting the precious metal from the rocks. Kalgoorlie quickly prospered, and the town's magnificent nineteenth-century public buildings, and streets wide enough to turn a camel train, remain as evidence of its fabulous wealth. Visitors flock to the town in September to enjoy the surrounding wildflowers.

Riding the groundswell at Wave Rock
Photo: Chris Mellor

WHERE
The Great Eastern Highway extends east from Perth to Kalgoorlie, in Western Australia. Wave Rock is about 150 kilometres south.

WHEN
NAIDOC (National Aboriginal & Islander Day of Celebration) week in September is a good time to visit Kalgoorlie, as the whole town celebrates this important festival with a parade, sporting events and traditional dancing. In early September the Kalgoorlie Racing Round, Western Australia's biggest outback horse-racing carnival, attracts thousands of punters and culminates in the 2300-metre Kalgoorlie Cup.

HOW
The visitors centre (08-9880 5182) in Hyden's Wave Rock Wildflower Shoppe has information on how to get to Mulka's Cave. Tours led by a Nyoongar guide depart daily from the shop, taking you on a short stroll to significant sites around Wave Rock.

Day trips from Perth that include Mulka's Cave and the Aboriginal-guided tour at Wave Rock are run by Australian Pinnacle Tours (1800 999 069).

In Kalgoorlie, the Aboriginal-owned Yamatji Bitja Aboriginal Bush Tours (08-9021 5862) runs highly recommended tours focusing on the heritage of the Wongi people. Try twilight tours with story-telling around a campfire, day trips that introduce you to bush skills, or overnight trips deep into traditional country.

The eclectic interior of the Spanish Benedictine church in New Norcia Photo: Peter Ptschelinzew

A Mystery Ship:
Great Northern Hwy

This great inland highway linking Perth and Port Hedland covers long stretches of semiarid outback country. Regularly pounded by long-haul road trains, this road has an atmosphere of its own. If you choose this route over the more popular coast road, you'll have the chance to see some off-beat attractions.

The monastery town of New Norcia is a cluster of ornate Spanish-style buildings incongruously set up in the Australian bush. Established by the Spanish Benedictine order in 1846 to proselytise among Yuat people, the monastery's work soon turned to raising Aboriginal orphans after European diseases ravaged the local communities.

Today it remains a working monastery running retreats and workshops. It also produces a range of boutique foods. The monastery's 100-year-old wood-fired oven turns out

sublime breads and cakes, and the locally pressed olive oil is heavenly. There's also an excellent museum here.

Further up the highway, 640 kilometres from Perth, is the historic town of Cue. The classic goldfields architecture here tells the story of the town's heyday during the 1890s gold rush. But long before this, the Cue region was a meeting and trading territory for Aboriginal people from all over Australia.

Wilgie Mia, northwest of Cue, might explain the area's prehistoric importance. This famous ochre quarry has been mined for up to 30,000 years. Aborigines used scaffolding, stone hammers and wooden wedges to remove thousands of tonnes of rock to get to the ochre, believed to have been traded as far away as Queensland. Today, however, visitors are discouraged from visiting Wilgie Mia for safety reasons.

The ancient Wilgie Mia ochre mine **Photo:** Peter Ptschelinzew

WHERE
Western Australia's Great
Northern Highway links
Perth and Port Hedland via
the inland route.

WHEN
Try to visit Cue during
QFest (www.qfest.com), a
four-day festival in October
featuring drag shows
(queens, not cars), music,
performance and the amaz-
ing Big Bell Sculpture
Burn – huge fire sculptures.

HOW
New Norcia Museum, Art
Gallery & Tourist Information Centre (08-9654
8056) details the town's
fascinating history.

The Cue Tourism Centre
(08-9963 1216) has
information on Aboriginal
experiences in the area.
Note that it is only open
from April until October.

Green with the envy: emeralds in the mining town of Cue **Photo:** Peter Ptschelinzew

Walga Rock (also known as Walganna), about forty-seven
kilometres southwest of Cue via Austin Downs Station, is a
rock monolith that juts fifty metres out of the surrounding
scrub. Walga, which means 'ochre painting' in the local
Warragi language, is one of the largest, best-preserved
painted art sites in Western Australia. The sixty-metre rock
shelter at the base of the rock houses a gallery of desert-
style paintings of lizards, birds and animals, and hand
stencils in red, white and yellow ochre.

At the northern end of the gallery, a ship with twin masts
and a funnel floating on four wavy lines has caused a lot of
debate. There's one theory that it was painted by ship-
wrecked sailors and another that a shearer did it, but like
many sites the story was never written and is now lost.

Ochre paintings at Walga Rock
Photo: Diana Mayfield

The days have just blended, time's irrelevant up here. The simplicity of the living is beautiful.

—Deb

A waterfall empties into Hancock Gorge in Karijini National Park **Photo:** Chris Bell

Spirit of the Range People: Central Ranges of WA

Kennedy Range, Mount Augustus and Karijini are three spectacular national parks that straddle the range country of central Western Australia. Mount Augustus is not only over 1700 million years old but twice the size of Uluru! This ancient landscape is popular with bushwalkers and, if you know where to look, there's rock art, *thalu* (ceremonial) sites and artefact scatters dating back at least 20,000 years.

The Kennedy Range is a huge mesa pushed up from a sea bed millions of years ago; fossilised sea shells can be seen in the cliffs. The southern and eastern sides have eroded to create dramatic 100-metre-high cliffs and canyons. The range is covered with red sand dunes and spinifex and forms the boundaries for the Maia and Malgaru peoples' country.

The national park here has over one hundred Aboriginal sites. There are a number of artefact scatters on the west-

ern side of the range, near the freshwater springs. Stone tools were made from the semiprecious coloured chert rock that forms the range's outcrops. Many of the park's sites have sacred significance: within the park, for example, is a March Fly *thalu* site where ceremonies were conducted to enhance the land's spiritual forces.

To the east, Mount Augustus (or Burringurrah as the local Wadjari people know it), is preserved in a national park. It's the biggest 'rock' in the world – twice as big as Uluru and three times as old – but it looks less dramatic because of partial vegetation cover. The granite underneath the layered rocks of the mount is estimated to be 1700 million years old.

There are Aboriginal engravings at three main sites: Ooramboo has engravings of animal tracks on a rock face;

Tufts of spinifex in Karijini National Park **Photo**: Richard I'Anson

Travelling the red roads of the Central Ranges **Photo**: Oliver Strewe

at Mundee the engravings are in a series of overhangs; and at Beedoboondu, the starting point for the climb to the summit, there are engravings of animal tracks and hunters.

Further north, Karijini National Park is rightly famous for its stunning gorges, waterfalls and beautiful swimming holes; wildflowers are an additional spring feature.

The excellent Karijini Visitors Centre is run by the traditional owners of Karijini, the Banyjima. It's a slick design that presents interpretive displays on the natural and cultural history of the park, along with a shop selling Aboriginal arts and crafts. The dramatic building represents a goanna and is designed to withstand the fires that are common in the area.

A flock of Corellas enjoying the view at Mount Augustus **Photo**: Diana Mayfield

WHERE

The range country covers a vast region of Western Australia. Kennedy Range National Park is 170 kilometres east of Carnarvon, Mount Augustus National Park is 280 kilometres further east and Karijini National Park is fifty kilometres east of Tom Price.

WHEN

Travelling can be difficult in the Wet (October to March), but if you come in spring (September to November) you'll be rewarded with wildflowers.

HOW

It's worth taking a tour to see these parks. Stockman Safaris (08-9941 2421), in Carnarvon, offers four-wheel-drive bush-experience tours to the Kennedy Ranges.

The Burringurrah community Aboriginal Corporation (08-9943 0979) offers a Mount Augustus walking tour, with a minimum of five people required. They also do bush tucker, hunting and women's business (no men allowed) tours. All tours begin at the Mount Augustus Outback Tourist Resort at the foot of the mountain.

Karijini Visitors Centre (08-9189 8121) is in the northeastern corner of Karijini National Park. The centre sometimes offers guided cultural activities.

Practising rodeo skills on a 44-gallon drum **Photo:** Richard I'Anson

Wild Heart:
Gibb River Rd

The rugged Gibb River Road (GRR) is one of Australia's great four-wheel-drive adventures. Faint-hearted tourists take the Great Northern Highway from Broome to Kununurra, but for those who want to see the 'real' Kimberley, the Gibb River Road is a great way to access its wild heart – not to mention getting a ripper tan on your driving arm. The 710-kilometre route crosses the traditional lands of the Ngarinyin people, a region made up of Aboriginal communities and cattle stations, and lots of open terrain.

As well as the world-famous Wandjina rock paintings (p178), this region is also famous for the Bradshaw figures, named after a European explorer who traversed the area in 1891 – the first nonindigenous person to see them. Generally small, the beautiful figures depict ethereal beings engaged in ceremonial, hunting or dance scenes. Some examples are 30,000 years old and much older than the

Wandjina, but both their source and their significance have largely been lost.

One of the delights of this trip is the chance to stay on a working cattle station. Many stations along the route offer dinner, bed and breakfast and the owners are in the best position to help you find the incredible rock art hidden away in secret corners of the Kimberley. A good bet is Mt Elizabeth Station. Alternatively, get yourself a swag, pop on a billy, stretch out under the stars and ask yourself: 'How's the serenity?'

The Mt Barnett Roadhouse, a major supply point along the route, is owned and run by the Kupungarri Aboriginal community. There are some Aboriginal art sites in this area to track down when you stop for a cuppa. The Mitchell Plateau (p176) is also well known for its Wandjina paintings.

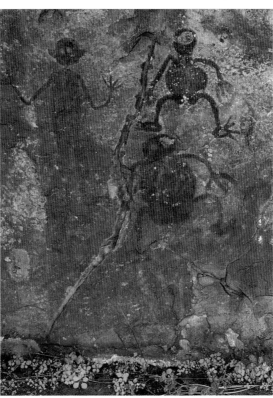

Rock paintings and wildflowers near the Gibb River Road **Photo:** Peter Ptschelinzew

Being in the bush is something I've been craving for a long time and it's doing my soul and my spirit wonders. It's loosening my shoulders and making the edges of my mouth curl up, makes me smile and laugh. — Cath

Big-bellied boab tree along the Gibb River Road **Photo:** John Banagan

WHERE
The Gibb River Road runs through the Kimberley from Derby to Kununurra. It forms an alternative route to the Great Northern Highway.

WHEN
The road opens during the Dry (May to November) and stays open until the weather breaks, whereupon you'll need a submarine, or at least a car with flippers. Roads close during the Wet and there are fines for disobeying restrictions.

HOW
This road is not a good idea for conventional vehicles or even unprepared four-wheel-drives, and two-wheel-drive campervans are definitely not recommended. Road conditions are posted daily at the Main Roads Western Australia website (www .mrwa.wa.gov.au). Derby Visitors Centre (08-9191 1426) and Kununurra Visitors Centre (08-9168 1177) also provide up-to-date information. The trip requires some careful planning, as there are only a handful of roadhouses along the way and no mobile-phone coverage. It's wise to carry several days' food and water in case you're stranded. Tour operators from Broome, Derby, Wyndham and Kununurra all offer four-wheel-drive tours along parts of the Gibb River Road.

Cath takes the plunge **Photo:** Peter Solness

Rock Heavies:
Bell Gorge

A freshwater oasis within the heart of the Kimberley in King Leopold National Park, Bell Gorge is pressed between the Isdell and King Leopold Ranges.

This is Wandjina country (p178), traditionally the land of the Ngarinyin people. In the surrounding hills, the mysterious, mouthless ancestor spirits have left their shadows on the rocks in the forms of rock paintings.

Featuring a series of tiered pools, a waterfall that runs even in the Dry and a dramatic clifftop backdrop, Bell Gorge offers a spectacular setting for a dip and has become a popular destination for travellers wanting to kick back, cool off and give their bones a chance to stop rattling.

Clean, sparkling water flows through a series of similar pools before dropping over a precipice into a wide, deep pool. Evil Knievel wannabees will enjoy the drop, though it's always a good idea to check water depth before plunging in. A 300-metre climb to the top of the cliff offers the best views. Rubber tyre tubes make great makeshift lilos if you have one handy.

It's thought that the surrounding King Leopold Range and Mitchell Plateau are one of the few mainland areas where there have been no flora or fauna extinctions since the advent of European settlement.

The rock layers that make up the Kimberley basin are over five kilometres thick (try digging a tunnel through that!) and date back 1900 million years to Precambrian times. The ranges were formed around 560 million years ago when rock layers found themselves rubbing shoulders with older volcanic rock heavies.

The smoking ceremony made me feel closer to the people of the country and the land. It's a ceremony forty thousand years old. And that makes me feel overwhelmed and extremely honoured. The Windjana spirit in the opening ceremony at the Sydney Olympic Games was a representation of the creator of all life that is Windjana. — Cath

Cath getting into the swim **Photo:** Peter Solness

Visitors wanting to stay overnight can pitch their tents by the old Silent Grove homestead, or stroll down to private camp sites where you can sleep beneath the shade of boab trees.

Deb shares a cuddle with the local kids
Photo: Peter Solness

WHERE
Bell Gorge, Western Australia, is 214 kilometres from Derby, around thirty kilometres off the Gibb River Road, in King Leopold National Park.

WHEN
The Dry (between April and September) is the best time to visit.

HOW
Admission to Bell Gorge is free. Depending on the weather, a ranger will collect a fee for camping. A number of tour operators visit Bell Gorge on tour itineraries, including Kimberley Wild (08-9193 7778).

Mighty *wandjinas* crowding the walls **Photo:** Mitch Reardon

The Mysterious Wandjina:
Windjana Gorge National Park

Surrounded by low-lying tussock-covered savannah in Bunuba country, the walls of Windjana Gorge jut abruptly from the landscape to a towering 100 metres in height. The gorge splices through the Napier Ranges, which formed an underwater limestone reef 350 million years ago during the Devonian period. Running through the three-and-a-half-kilometre gorge is the Lennard River, a raging torrent in the Wet that transforms into sleepy sandbanks dotted with fresh-water billabongs and patches of boab trees during the Dry.

The gorge is bursting with paperbark trees, broad-leaved Leich-hardt pines and native figs that are home to corellas and fruit bats. Down by the pools are freshwater crocodiles sunbaking on sandbanks. If you camp at night, shine a torch down to the billabongs and you'll be greeted with the sight of lots of pairs of eyes blinking right back at you from the water. The crocs are not considered harmful unless deliberately aggravated.

The gorge contains a cave depicting the *wandjina*, the mysterious ancestor spirits who have left their shadows on the rock in the form of world-famous rock paintings. These Creator beings of the Dreaming who came from the sky and sea have the power to summon the Wet's storms. You'll recognise them by their mouthless faces, which feature large eyes, a beakish nose and a head surrounded by a halo of lines representing hair and lightning, which is under the *wandjina*'s control. Traditionally, each *wandjina* had its own custodian family who retouched the paintings annually. These beings hold a unique place in Aboriginal spiritual life, and sites depicting them are sacred.

Around fifty kilometres away is Tunnel Creek National Park. Here the creek has literally tunnelled itself under the Napier Ranges to the Oscar Ranges. You can explore the 750-metre tunnel, which is hung with bats and lined with pools;

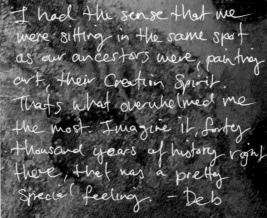

I had the sense that we were sitting in the same spot as our ancestors were, painting art, their Creation Spirit. That's what overwhelmed me the most. Imagine it, forty thousand years of history right there, that was a pretty special feeling. – Deb

Cath and Deb investigate rock art with Dillon Andrews Photo: Peter Solness

occasionally a distant splash will remind you that you are not alone... A roof collapse halfway through helps illuminate the tunnel, though you'll still need to bring a torch. Note that Aboriginal women are forbidden to enter the caves.

These caves are particularly significant to the Bunuba because of Jandamarra (also known as Pigeon for his ability to 'fly' away and disappear), a Bunuba resistance leader who hid out here for three years until he was caught and killed in 1887.

There are various versions of the story, but essentially Jandamarra was active in the region at a time when local people were being pushed from their lands due to pastoral activities. As a young man Jandamarra was picked up and imprisoned for spearing a sheep. Later he became an unofficial tracker for the police outpost based at Lillimooloora, helping to track his own tribespeople. Eventually Jandamarra's tribal loyalties got the better of him. He shot a constable dead, stole some guns, set the prisoners free and escaped to the caves. The Bunuba people, who admired and feared him, thought Jandamarra had magical powers and was a physical manifestation of a spirit living near Tunnel Creek. Eventually he was killed by an indigenous tracker called Micki from the Pilbara region. It is said that his head was severed and sent in a jar to England and has never been seen since. Jandamarra is now a folk hero to the Bunuba people along the lines of the Apache resistance leader Geronimo.

Below, from top: Deb and Cath with kids at Windjana Gorge; Dillon Andrews, local tour guide; Painted kids at Biridu camp in the Leopold Ranges
Photos: Peter Solness

WHERE
Windjana Gorge National Park is 130 kilometres northwest of Fitzroy, 140 kilometres southeast of Derby, in Western Australia.

WHEN
The Dry (between April and September) is the best time to visit. The road is often closed from December to March.

HOW
Camping is allowed in Windjana Gorge National Park, but check with the Derby Visitors Centre (08-9191 1426) for road conditions before setting out.

Bungoolee Tours (08-9191 5257/5633), founded by Bunuba local Dillon Andrews, offers two-day trips to Windjana Gorge, Tunnel Creek, the ruins of Lillimooloora Station and Jandamarra's hide-out. It's the best way to get an Aboriginal perspective of the landscape and its history.

Indigenous Art

Visual imagery is a fundamental part of indigenous life –
a connection between past and present, between the
supernatural and the earthly, between people and the land.
The visual arts fulfil educational, spiritual and social roles
for Aboriginal Australians. For indigenous artists, the object
produced is secondary to the process, as the production
of paintings, carvings and woven products reinforces the
Aboriginal way of life: their customs, stories and practical
requirements.

The early forms of indigenous artistic expression include
rock carvings, ceremonial body painting, ground designs,
rock engravings and wood-burnt design. All early indigenous
art was based on the various clans' and nations' ancestral
Dreamings – the Creation – when the earth's physical
features were formed by the struggles between powerful
supernatural ancestors such as the Rainbow Serpent, the
Lightning Men and the Wandjina (p178). Today there is a
huge range of material being produced across Australia,
including paintings, batik and wood carvings from central
Australia, bark paintings from Arnhem Land, ironwood
carvings and silk-screen printing from the Tiwi Islands,
and didjeridus. While the art of the more traditional
communities differs in style from urban works, a common
theme that runs through all the works is the strong and
ancient connection that indigenous people have with the
land. Through art indigenous people have found a way of
voicing identity and renewing indigenous culture and the
spirit of the Dreaming.

In recent times, various indigenous art forms have
undergone significant change, reflecting shifting social and
political environments. In the late 1920s, missionaries
encouraged the production of art as saleable items,
with the aim of providing indigenous communities with
the means for a self-sustaining economic venture while
reinforcing Aboriginal identity in the face of an increasingly
dominant European environment. The commercial demands
for Aboriginal art led to works being produced using
nontraditional colours and media, and a shift away from
sacred or secret designs towards direct representation.

Rock Art

The ancient outdoor galleries found throughout Australia
are precious records of indigenous Australian culture.
Some rock paintings are believed to date back between
18,000 and 60,000 years and provide a record of changing
environments and lifestyles over the millennia. For the local

Aboriginal people the rock-art sites are a major source of traditional knowledge – they are historical archives in place of a written form.

Rock paintings show how the main styles succeeded each other over time. The earliest hand or grass prints were followed by a naturalistic style, with large outlines of people or animals filled in with colour. Then came the dynamic style, in which motion was often depicted (a dotted line, for example, to show a spear's path through the air). In this era the first mythological beings appeared, with human bodies and animal heads. Following this was a style featuring simple human silhouettes and then the more recent X-ray style, which displays the internal organs and bone structure of animals.

The paintings of Arnhem Land in the Northern Territory constitute one of the world's most important and fascinating rock-art collections. They range from hand prints (a form of artist signature) to paintings of animals, some of which, such as the thylacine (Tasmanian tiger), have long been extinct on the Australian mainland; people, including Makasar traders from what is now Sulawesi; mythological beings; and European ships. Two of the finest sites are open to visitors: Ubirr (p139) and Nourlangie (p140) in Kakadu National Park.

The rock art of the Kimberley is perhaps best known for its images of the Wandjina, a group of Ancestral Beings who came from the sky and sea and were associated with fertility. The Wandjina paintings are the shadows of Ancestors, imprinted on the rock as they pass by. These Ancestral Beings controlled the elements and were responsible for the formation of the country's features. They generally appear in human form, with large black eyes, a nose but no mouth, a halo around the head (representative of both hair and clouds) and a black oval shape on the chest. Some of these rock images are more than seven metres long. Each Wandjina traditionally has its own custodian family, and to ensure good relations between the Wandjina and the people, the images have to be retouched annually.

In north Queensland the Quinkan rock-art galleries near Laura (p154) are among the best known in the country. Among the creatures depicted on the walls are the Quinkan spirits, which are shown in two forms – the long and stick-like Timara, and the crocodile-like Imjim with their knobbed, club-like tails.

Painting

Western Desert painting, also known as dot painting, is probably the most well known of indigenous painting styles. It partly evolved from 'ground paintings', which formed the centrepiece of dances and songs. These were made from pulped plant material, with designs made on the ground. While dot paintings may look random and abstract, they depict Dreaming stories and can be read in many ways, including as aerial landscape maps. Many paintings feature the tracks of birds, animals and humans, often identifying the land's ancestral beings. Subjects may be depicted by the imprint they leave in the sand – a simple arc depicts a person (as that is the print left by someone sitting cross-legged); a coolamon (wooden carrying dish) is shown by an oval shape; a digging stick by a single line; and a campfire by a circle. Men or women are identified by the objects associated with them: digging sticks and coolamons for women, spears and boomerangs for men. Concentric circles usually depict Dreaming sites, or places where ancestors paused in their journeys.

While these symbols are widely used, their meaning in each individual painting is known only by the artist and the people closely associated with them – either by clan or by the Dreaming – since different clans apply different interpretations to each painting. In this way sacred stories can be publicly portrayed, as the deeper meaning is not revealed to uninitiated viewers.

Bark painting, using the bark of the stringy-bark tree, is an integral part of the cultural heritage of Arnhem Land indigenous people. It's difficult to establish when bark was first used, partly because it is perishable, so very old pieces don't exist. The paintings were never intended to be permanent records. One of the main features of these paintings is the use of *rarrk* (crosshatching) designs. These designs identify the particular clans, and are based on body paintings handed down through generations. In the region images tend to be naturalistic and are set on plain backgrounds, while in the east geometric, abstract designs predominate.

The art reflects Dreaming themes that vary by region. In eastern Arnhem Land the prominent Ancestor Beings are the Djang'kawu Sisters, who travelled the land with elaborate dilly (carry) bags and digging sticks to make water holes, and the Wagilag Sisters, who are associated with snakes and water holes. In western Arnhem Land, Yingarna,

the Rainbow Serpent, is the significant being, as is one of her offspring, Ngalyod. Other groups paint Nawura as the main Ancestral Being; he travelled through the rocky landscape creating sacred sites and giving people the attributes of culture. The Mimi spirits also feature in western Arnhem Land art, both on bark and rock. These mischievous spirits are believed to have taught the indigenous people of the region many skills, such as hunting, food gathering and painting.

Artefacts & Crafts

Objects traditionally made for practical or ceremonial uses, such as boomerangs and didjeridus, often featured intricate and symbolic decoration. Wooden sculptures (of birds, fish, animals and ancestral beings) were traditionally produced for particular ceremonies, and were engraved and painted with intricate symbolic designs.

Also popular are the woodcarvings that have designs scorched into them with hot fencing wire. These range from small figures such as possums to quite large snakes and lizards. Many are connected with Dreaming stories from the artists' country. Tiwi artists create impressive carvings from ironwood, said to be impossible for termites to bore through.

Articles made from fibres are a major art form among indigenous women, although in some regions men also made woven objects that they used as hunting tools. String or twine was traditionally made from bark, grass, leaves, roots and other materials, hand-spun and dyed with natural pigments, then woven to make dilly bags, baskets, garments, fishing nets and other items. Strands or fibres from the leaves of the pandanus palm (and other palms or grasses) were also woven to make dilly bags and mats.

While all these objects have utilitarian purposes, many also have ritual uses. As well as their customary use, many items are produced specifically for sale to the tourist market. Some communities also specialise in producing nontraditional pieces such as engraved emu eggs and boab nuts.

Many excellent contemporary artworks are available for sale. The best place to buy them is either directly from the communities' art centres or from galleries that are owned and operated by indigenous communities. Reputable galleries are usually members of the Australian Commercial Galleries Association (ACGA). Buying indigenous art in this way promotes an autonomous and authentic arts industry for Aboriginal Australians.

Dipping a toe in the Fitzroy River **Photo:** Peter Solness

Floods & Fords: Fitzroy Crossing

Driving east from Derby, you'll eventually see a faint bump appear on an otherwise flat horizon: welcome to Fitzroy Crossing, population 1500.

Aboriginal people have lived around Fitzroy Crossing for thousands of years and there are more than thirty Aboriginal communities scattered around Fitzroy Valley.

This area was the site of fierce indigenous resistance, the best-known leader being the Bunuba police tracker-turned-freedom fighter Jandamarra (p179). In fact, Aborigines managed to create so much trouble in these parts that in 1900 around a quarter of the Western Australian police force was based in the Kimberley. Some might say this was overkill.

A town first sprang up here in 1897 because it was a convenient spot to ford the Fitzroy River. The first bridge

was built in 1935, but even so the floods were sometimes so high that travellers had to take a flying fox (a cable mechanism) instead.

Back in 1890 Joseph Blyth built the Crossing Inn, now the oldest pub in the Kimberley. It still has a lively atmosphere (as the avalanche of beer cans beside it suggests) and a shady spot on the veranda to crack a coldie. Another thing that hasn't changed are the seasons. During the Wet the river can rise up to ten metres and flood the plain for fifteen kilometres, turning Fitzroy Crossing into an island.

In town, visitors should check out the Mangkaja Arts Centre, which stocks baskets, souvenirs and paintings. Established in the 1980s to help foster traditional culture, employment, fair trade and pride in Aboriginal identity, the arts cooperative has produced some of the Kimberley's

Cath and I had to go down to the river and stick our feet in water and walk along the sand. We actually ran into a mob down there that was sitting around the campfire fishing. That was Danny Marr, from Fitzroy Express, a legend country-rock band here in the Kimberly. He told us about his life, his work and his music and he sang us a song, 'Rodeo Road'. By the end of it Cath and I were shouting out the chorus along with his daughters, nieces and nephews. — Deb

WHERE
Fitzroy Crossing is 392 kilometres east of Broome and 258 kilometres south-east of Derby, in Western Australia.

WHEN
The best time to visit is during the Dry, between April and September, as the road to Fitzroy Crossing is sometimes flooded in the Wet.

HOW
The Fitzroy Crossing Tourism Bureau (08-9191 5355) is on the main highway. The Darlngunaya Backpackers (08-9191 5140) is an Aboriginal-owned business that also offers bike and canoe hire. Darngku Heritage Cruises (08-9191 5552) has Aboriginal interpretive tours of Geikie Gorge. They cover the region's flora, fauna and cultural traditions and include a nature walk and a hunt for bush foods.

best-known artists, including Nyuju Stumpy Brown, Butcher Cherel, Paji Honeychild Yankarr and Ngarralja Tommy May.

Fitzroy Crossing is also a good base for exploring the surrounding area, including the beautiful Geikie Gorge National Park, known as Darngku to the Bunuba. A mere eighteen kilometres away, the park is home to harmless Johnson crocodiles, sawfish and freshwater stringrays whose ancestors swam through the ancient saltwater reef in Devonian times. If you're feeling lazy you might like to cast a line for barramundi in the shade of the river that's closer to town.

Equally fascinating in this region is the vegetation. Along the road from Derby to Fitzroy Crossing, you'll pass through bush dotted with African boab trees from Madagascar. How the boabs wound up in Western Australia is a bit of a mystery, but there are theories aplenty. Some say the nuts of the boab floated across the Indian Ocean and washed up on the Western Australia coastline. Other theories involve ancient trade routes, while the more imaginative describe Australia and Madagascar rubbing shoulders as part of the ancient supercontinent of Gondwanaland.

A quiet smile
Photo: Peter Solness

Real-life cowboy and Deb and Cath looking the part at the Halls Creek Rodeo **Photo:** Tony Jackson

Cowboys & Craters: Halls Creek

The Kimberley is mostly populated by townships of the 'blink and you'll miss it' variety. In this context, a place like Halls Creek, which boasts a township of almost 1600 people, passes for a thriving metropolis. Perched on the edge of the Great Sandy Desert and adjacent to the Great Northern Highway, the town is surrounded by desert hills covered in tufts of spinifex.

Today Halls Creek is predominantly an Aboriginal settlement, with Jaru, Kidja, and Grooniyandi communities living nearby. Prior to white settlement, Aborigines lived a nomadic hunting and gathering life based around local water holes.

The original township of Halls Creek was founded around 1885 when two explorers, Charles Hall (who gave his name to the town) and Jack Slattery, discovered gold at the Elvire

River. The gold rush gave birth to the requisite mod cons, such as a post office, two hotels and a couple of humpies (bark huts).

In 1955, with the gold rush over, the townsfolk voted to up sticks and move the village fifteen kilometres to the northwest. The new site was in less hospitable country but conveniently located next to the Great Northern Highway (p170). Now a ghost town, the old township's most interesting feature is its strange post office made from spinifex and termite mounds.

Following the gold rush, pastoral activities took off as the main local industry. Indigenous people started working on pastoral stations for white people, or *gardiyas* as they're known, in return for basic rations such as flour, sugar and blankets. Some were coerced into working on the stations,

Cath and Deb riding ahead of a cattle muster bound for Halls Creek **Photo:** Peter Solness

while others were drawn to them. The system died out in the 1970s with the introduction of equal wages and the right to vote for Aboriginal people. During these days, Halls Creek was the last ration and supply stop for any thirsty stockmen embarking on the infamous 2000-kilometre-long Canning Stock Route (p110).

Halls Creek continues its tradition as a meeting place with its annual rodeo. As the event draws near the town steels itself for the influx of stock-men arriving from hundreds of kilometres around, some of whom have been in the bush for six months or more, and are eager for some yee-har. The event is as popular with indigenous stockmen as it is with their whitefella counterparts.

Halls Creek is definitely a rodeo with a difference. Forget the dagwood dogs, blasting stereo systems and cheesy souvenirs – everyone at the rodeo is there for one reason, and that's to participate and hopefully go home with a famed belt-buckle prize. Needless to say, big hats, Cuban heels and

Cowboy Jae Long of Halls Creek rides saddle bronc
Photo: Kim Hamblin

Cattle muster amidst the dust en route to Halls Creek **Photo:** Peter Solness

cowboy shirts are *de rigueur*. You'll see jillaroos (female trainees on a station) competing in equestrian events such as barrel races, and kids as young as three trying their luck riding poddy (handfed) calves. But the undisputed highlights of the event are the wild-horse bareback ride (also known as 'suicide ride') and the feature bull ride, which sees contestants mount a two-tonne hunk of 100 per cent mean beef cattle. It's from zero to hero if you can last the mandatory eight seconds; many luckless riders owe their life to the fearless rodeo clowns who take the heat when they bite the dust.

In town, don't miss the nonprofit Yarliyil Arts Centre, showcasing works by artists based on local Dreaming stories. Close by, the Billiluna Aboriginal community invites tourists to visit for bushwalking, bird-watching and fishing at nearby Lake Gregory.

Halls Creek also makes a great jumping-off point for local attractions such as Purnululu National Park and Wolfe Creek Crater (p121), the China Wall fault line and the Palm Springs freshwater oasis.

WHERE
Halls Creek, Western
Australia, is around 2800
kilometres northeast of
Perth and 1200 kilometres
southeast of Darwin.

WHEN
The Dry, between April
and September, is the best
time to visit. The rodeo is
usually held in July – check
with the tourist office for
exact dates.

HOW
Halls Creek Tourist Office
(08-9168 6262) can
organise accommodation
and tours to surrounding
attractions between April
and October. Billiluna
Aboriginal community
(08-9168 8988) offers day
activities and camping is
available; visitors must call
for permission beforehand.

My dad was a
cowboy. I'm really
looking forward to
smelling the horses
and seeing the dust
fly off the spurs.
It's going to stir
up a lot of things
for me again. —Deb.

Two lonesome cowgirls standing by at Halls Creek Rodeo
Photo: Tony Jackson

Ruins of the wireless station on Telegraph Hill which once assisted ships entering Wyndham Port Photo: Peter Ptschelinzew

Crocodile Country: Wyndham

As you drive through the dust and searing sun into the unusual outback town of Wyndham, you'll be welcomed by the gaping jaws of a twenty-metre concrete crocodile. Visitors take note: you are now entering serious croc country. Prehistoric and quietly awe-inspiring, these creatures are an obsession in this small town and an integral part of Wyndham's folklore.

Renowned for its scorching heat and surrounded by saltpans and mud flats, Wyndham is fortunately situated at the confluence of five rivers – the King, Pentecost, Durack, Forrest and Ord – and perched on the banks of the Cambridge Gulf.

With a population of just over 1000, Wyndham feels like a ghost town. But this quiet veneer belies its colourful history. By 1886, Wyndham, which was originally inhabited by the Djeidji, Dulngari and Aruagga people, had become a rollicking port full of Chinese miners and Afghan traders servicing

the gold rush at Halls Creek (p186). This was an era when outback legends were born – such as the one about how inventive Aborigines shimmied up the poles of the Overland Telegraph Line when it arrived in 1889, to harvest the line's ceramic insulators as spearheads. When the gold dried up, Wyndham's fortune dwindled and it settled into a modest supporting role supplying the cattle stations of the eastern Kimberley; it still exports live cattle to Asia today.

Much of the original character of the town has been retained, no doubt because the old (port) area, which still reeks of the days when horses and carts rattled down the street, is a few kilometres from the newer hub of town, known as Three Mile. The remoteness of Wyndham means uninterrupted, breathtaking views, especially at dawn and dusk. The Five Rivers Lookout reveals one of the most dramatic vistas of the Australian coastline. Another natural wonder, albeit a quirky one,

Just a baby at Wyndham Crocodile Farm Photo: Bella Kenworthy

WHERE
Wyndham is in Western Australia, 3450 kilometres northeast of Perth and 105 kilometres northwest of Kununurra.

WHEN
Temperatures are lower and access is easier in Australia's winter months (June to August). Many roads are closed in the Wet (January to April) and the mozzies are ferocious during this period.

HOW
The gregarious Morgan family run Wundargoodie Aboriginal Safaris (0429 928 088) offers customised cultural and fishing tours, with insights into Aboriginal life and culture, bush tucker and the flora and fauna of the Kimberley.

is the Prison Tree, a hollowed-out old boab tree on King River Road, which police once used as a temporary holding cell.

Another unmissable sight is the striking Warriu Dreamtime Park statues. These enormous copper sculptures depicting an Aboriginal family and native fauna were presented to Wyndham by the Jarook Ngarni Aboriginal community for the 1988 Bicentennial (which commemorated the 200th anniversary of permanent European settlement in Australia). Towering and mythical, they shimmer against the blue sky.

Wyndham is a northern gateway to the Gibb River Road (p174) and the access point to two of Australia's most intriguing and isolated Aboriginal settlements – the former mission towns of Kalumburu and Oombulgurri. Permits are required to visit either town.

The croc-heavy waters of Oombulgurri spawned Oombi, Wyndham Crocodile Farm's resident saltwater bad boy, notorious for eating approximately twenty-six of the community's dogs. Australia is home to the largest species of salties, and locals take precautions to avoid being on the menu. Some Aboriginal communities protect visitors to their country with a smoking ritual believed to give protection from the crocs.

So as you leave Wyndham, take a last look at that concrete Big Croc in your rear view mirror. Enormous, unique and just a bit scary – not unlike the landscape around Wyndham itself.

Below, from top: Cath takes a scenic flight; Evening descends on Wyndham pier Photos: Bella Kenworthy.

Boab trees silhouetted against a fiery Kununurra sunset **Photo:** Richard I'Anson

Something in the Water: Kununurra

How appropriate: in the local Miriwoong language, Kununurra (the European version of Gananoorrang) means 'meeting of big waters'. Water abounds in this upbeat new town where crops prosper (check out the mangoes in November) and waterways are works of engineering genius.

The town was founded in 1960 as the centre for the Ord River Irrigation Scheme – an ambitious programme designed to harness the area's water for agriculture, which has resulted in an intriguing ecosystem of rivers, wetlands and lakes, and created the Kimberley's most verdant town.

Flanked by both Lily Creek Lagoon and the diminutive Mirima National Park, Kununurra sits close to the Western Australia–Northern Territory border, making it a logical entry point for the Top End and a perfect gateway to the highlights of the eastern Kimberley, including Purnululu

National Park (p120) and the northeastern end of the Gibb River Road (p174).

Mirima National Park, just northeast of Kununurra, is of great significance to the Miriwoong people as part of their Head Lice Dreaming and contains ancient rock art and axe-grinding grooves. While most of the park is made up of spinifex plains dotted with boab trees, the twisted sandstone gorges of Hidden Valley with their banded rock formations have been likened to a mini-Bungle Bungle Range.

Not only is the region physically lush, but creatively it throbs with life too. Without doubt, one of the best examples is the Jirrawun Aboriginal Art Corporation. Formed in the mid-1990s, Jirrawun (meaning 'one') is a group of Gija Elders from the Warmun region, 200 kilometres south of Kununurra, many of whom worked originally as stockmen

Jirrawun artist Freddie Timms at work **Photo:** Bella Kenworthy

WHERE
Kununurra is in Western Australia, 1050 kilometres east of Broome and 800 kilometres southwest of Darwin.

WHEN
Most visitors come in the Dry (May to September).

HOW
For a good introduction to the Kimberley art aesthetic of the Jirrawun artists and others in the area, visit one of the several good galleries in town. Red Rock Art Gallery (08-9169 3000) is a stylish space showcasing a range of paintings, metal sculptures and basketwork. Waringarri Aboriginal Arts centre (08-9168 2212) includes many paintings made with local ochres and pigments.

Kimberley Specialists (08-9168 2576) offers an intriguing mix of sustainable tourism and indigenous culture. Many of its tours are led by charismatic Miriwoong Elder Ju Ju Wilson.

and took up painting on canvas only in their retirement. Their works are renowned for large blocks of colour and abstract shapes that evoke the sheer scale and pared-back grandeur of their country. Although completely contemporary in appearance, the paintings are rich in the lore of family Dreamings, traditional stories and oral histories – not least the infamous Bedford Downs Massacre. The massacre took place in 1924 when an attempted spearing of the station owners resulted in the owners serving poisoned stew to all the indigenous people living nearby.

Members of Jirrawun include Freddie Timms, Paddy Bedford, Phyllis Thomas and Rusty Peters. Paddy Bedford's work is about to go global, permanently gracing the ground floor of the new Musée du Quai Branly (showcasing art from Africa, Asia, Oceania and the Americas) on the banks of the Seine in Paris. Not bad for a man hitting his artistic prime as he approaches his mid-eighties.

Truly, there is something in the water in Kununurra.

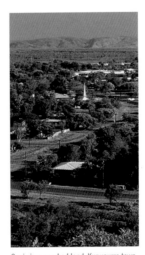

Oasis in a parched land: Kununurra town
Photo: Richard I'Anson

Take a cruise or canoe trip between the quartzite walls of magnificent Katherine Gorge Photo: Chris Mellor

Cicada Dreaming: Katherine

As you're cruising along the Stuart Highway in the Northern Territory, keep cruising and cruising and cruising. Eventually you will find the highway has become Katherine Terrace and yes, you're now in Katherine, population 6720, home to the Jawoyn, Dagoman and Wardaman people.

The town itself is a bit of a one-street pony, albeit a fairly modern one with all the requisite conveniences and a little kick to it. The Katherine Museum gives a fascinating insight into the region's modern history, and the School of the Air (which educates children from remote communities) boasts the world's largest classrooms. But most people aren't here for the township as much as for its proximity to some natural pearls of the indigenous landscape.

One of the Northern Territory's biggest drawcards is Nitmiluk National Park, a 3000-square-kilometre reserve

that contains the spectacular Katherine Gorge – twelve kilometres of sheer sandstone beauty carved out by the Katherine River. The gorge was formed between twenty and twenty-five million years ago, and it is, in fact, thirteen gorges (all neatly numbered) separated by rapids of varying lengths. However you slice and dice it, Nitmiluk is a wonderland to walk, swim (only the shy freshwater crocodiles here), canoe or camp in.

'Nitmiluk' means 'Cicada Dreaming' in Jawoyn. Title to the land was handed back to the Jawoyn people in 1989, and they now lease it to a government body while retaining traditional rights over the area so as to allow hunting, food gathering and ceremonies to continue. Bolung, the Rainbow Serpent, is said to reside in the pools of the second gorge, so there are rules attached to swimming, fishing and drinking the water there.

In the western corner of the park are the picturesque Leliyn Falls (Edith Falls), which cascade through several plunge pools that are perfect for swimming before dropping into the pandanus-lined – and aptly named – Sweetwater Pool. To make the most of a dip, take a hike on the Leliyn Walk, which climbs into escarpment country through grevillea and spinifex and past scenic lookouts on its way to the Upper Pool.

While Nitmiluk lies on Aboriginal land, there's little opportunity to interact with Aboriginal people in the park, so many visitors are drawn to the community of Manyallaluk, which is named after a nearby Frog Dreaming site and lies just outside the park's eastern boundary. Mayali and Ngalkbun people operate a mainstream tourism programme here with one-day tours that include, among other things, a bush-tucker lunch by a spring-fed swimming hole and lessons in traditional crafts. Try your hand at painting with ochres, weaving a basket, playing a didjeridu, fire-lighting and spear-throwing.

West of Katherine in Wardaman country is the Yingalarri Waterhole, a stunning rock-art site. The rock paintings and engravings here feature the Lightning Brothers, who are responsible for the wet season's violent storms that help the land to regenerate.

Below, from top: Catherine in Katherine;
The girls take a refreshing dip
Photos: Peter Solness

WHERE
Katherine is in the Northern Territory, 320 kilometres south of Darwin on the Stuart Highway. Nitmiluk National Park is thirty kilometres northeast of Katherine on a sealed road. The Leliyn Falls turn-off is forty kilometres north of Katherine on the Stuart Highway and the falls a further twenty kilometres on a sealed road. The Manyalla-luk turn-off is fifty kilometres southwest of Katherine on the Stuart Highway. The community is a further fifty kilometres north, much of it on unsealed road.

WHEN
Most visitors prefer the cooler dry season (May to September), when the waters of the gorge are calm. During the Wet (November to April) they can become a raging torrent and boating, canoeing and swimming are restricted. Manyallaluk is closed to visitors in the Wet.

HOW
The best place to find out about Jawoyn law and culture is at the Nitmiluk National Park visitors centre (08-8972 1886). Travel North (www.travel north.com.au) has a monopoly on tours in the park.

Traditional owner Ryan Baruwei (08-8975 4203) offers guided walks around Leliyn Falls on an ancient Jawoyn trading route. Tours to Manyallaluk can be booked on 08-8975 4727.

Paintings adorning a cave wall at Mangana Photo: Ross Barnett

Limestone Legends: Atherton Tableland

Edge-of-the-outback Chillagoe may only be three hours' drive from the Queensland coast, but it's a long way from the commercialisation of Cairns or the glam of Port Douglas. A visit offers a glimpse into life in the outback, and a chance to see the fabulous Aboriginal rock-art galleries in nearby Mungana.

The area around Chillagoe is a strange landscape of limestone karst formations protecting remnant stands of rainforest. Over seventy-five species of birds make their home in this oasis from the open woodland of the surrounding plains. Below ground, a series of beautiful limestone caves can be explored.

The Aboriginal rock-art galleries are in Chillagoe-Mungana Caves National Park, west of the Atherton Tableland. The Wullumba art site, also known as Balancing Rock, is a shel-

ter where incisions in the rock face have been deepened by successive occupants. Naturally occurring red ochre and white clay have been used to daub symbols, which were probably last repainted 100 years ago and are now quite weathered.

The art at Mungana is in a beautiful site among the extraordinary karst limestone formations of the park. Motifs include freehand drawings of lizard-like creatures in white ochre. Take the dirt road west of Chillagoe towards Mungana for fifteen kilometres, then turn off for Royal Arch Caves. The site is right next to the road, about two kilometres along.

About 130 kilometres southeast is the town of Ravenshoe, a forestry centre on the edge of the Tableland and home to the largest wind farm in Australia. Here you'll find

The buttressed trunk of a fig tree fans upwards from the forest floor Photo: Paul Dymond

WHERE
Chillagoe is 210 kilometres west of Cairns in Far North Queensland. Ravenshoe is 150 kilometres south of Cairns.

WHEN
The last twenty-five kilometres of the road to Chillagoe is unsealed, so if you're in a two-wheel drive it's better to make the trip in the Dry (April to December) and the best time is June to August.

HOW
Drop by the Queensland Parks & Wildlife Service (07-4094 7163) in Chillagoe for detailed maps and information on self-guided cave trails in Chillagoe-Mungana Caves National Park. The rangers also run interesting guided tours.

Plenty of companies offer day trips from Cairns, or try Chillagoe Cabins (07-4094 7206), which runs four-wheel-drive tours.

Explore the rainforest lifestyle of the Jirrbal people at the Ravenshoe (Koombooloomba) Visitor Centre (07-4097 7700), where you can see a palm-leaf shelter and learn how to prepare poisonous black-bean seeds so that they are safe for eating.

information on the local Jirrbal people and their relationship with the rainforest at the visitors centre and the Wabunga Wayemba Rainforest Walkabout.

A furrowed field darkens beneath a stormy sky
Photo: Sally Dillon

197

Streamside rocks and ferns in the Carnarvon Gorge **Photo:** Chris Bell

Tunnel Tombs:
Carnarvon National Park

Stunning Carnarvon Gorge is an oasis of sandstone cliffs, moss gardens, deep pools and rare palms in the dry plains. It's no wonder Aboriginal people spent time here. They left superb artwork – a highlight of a visit to the park – as well as an ancient burial ground.

Baloon Cave is an easily accessible overhang that catches the morning sun in winter. The cave features hand and axe stencils (*baloon* is a local word for axe – rock from the cave was possibly used to make stone axes).

The site called the Art Gallery is a spectacular assemblage of stencils, engravings and freehand paintings. There are three freehand drawings of white goannas here and at the far end of the gallery are hundreds of engravings, including a nest of emu eggs, a ten-metre serpent and the paw-print of an unknown, five-toed animal. However, the ancient art-

ists had a particular enthusiasm for engraving vulvas – there are more here than anywhere else in Australia!

Cathedral Cave is a massive overhang decorated with numerous stencils and freehand ochre paintings dating back some 3500 years. A freehand spirit figure, unique in the area, has pride of place. Elsewhere, panels of repeated boomerang stencils indicate that a group of hunters used the site; and stencils of oval *che-ka-ra* (*melo*-shell pendants), which originated in Cape York, tell the story of trade between tribes.

In the Mount Moffatt section of the park is an eerie place known as the Tombs, a network of natural tunnels that once formed an Aboriginal burial ground dating back 9400 years. Skeletons wrapped in decorated bark cylinders were discovered here in the nineteenth century.

A spectacular sinuous canyon in Carnarvon Gorge Photo: Chris Bell

WHERE
Carnarvon National Park is in the middle of the Great Dividing Range, between Roma and Emerald, a ten-hour drive from Brisbane, Queensland.

WHEN
The cooler months (April to October) are the best time to visit.

HOW
There are parks offices at Carnarvon Gorge (07-4984 4505) and Mount Moffatt (07-4626 3581).

In the winter months, Sunrover Expeditions (07-3203 4241) runs a six-day four-wheel-drive tour from Brisbane to Carnarvon Gorge, which includes a full-day walk to the Art Gallery and Cathedral Cave.

The Community Development Employment Programme (CDEP) Aboriginal Workshop (07-4654 3016) in Charleville offers tours of their workshop, parts of which are painted with traditional motifs, with an enthusiastic guide.

During a Charleville sightseeing tour with Fabulous Outback Escapes (07-4654 1114) you can follow the creation of a didjeridu, from cutting and debarking to seeing it being painted in the CDEP Aboriginal Workshop and finally hearing it played after a beeswax mouthpiece is added.

While in this region, it's well worth making the trip to Charleville to take in the Community Development Employment Programme (CDEP) Aboriginal Workshop, which sells a good range of art and handicrafts and offers tours.

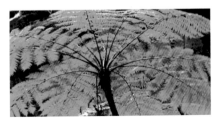

A tree fern's umbrella-like crown
Photo: Chris Bell

Stenciled ochre drawings at the Art Gallery
Photo: Richard I'Anson

Shearers' quarters at Thunderbolts Way, named after bushranger and local hero Captain Thunderbolt **Photo:** Ian Connellan

Fine Art & Country Music: New England Region

Sitting atop the Great Diving Range, the New England table-land is a vast landscape of sheep- and cattle-grazing with a burgeoning adventure-sports scene. This is also the spiritual home of Australian country music. Aboriginal artists such as Jimmy Little and Troy Cassar-Daley have helped to define the sound of Australian country that finds its greatest expression at the Tamworth Country Music Festival in late January.

The area is rich in indigenous heritage. At Armidale you can visit the Aboriginal Cultural Centre & Keeping Place to immerse yourself in the mystic qualities of Aboriginal art, or head to nearby Mount Yarrowyck to see a red-ochre rock painting. The markings could be bird tracks, eggs or even human figures.

To the northwest, on the way to Moree, the Myall Creek memorial is a sombre reminder of the massacre of twenty-eight

Wirrayaraay women, children and old men that occurred here in June 1838. You can bring a stone from your own area as a pilgrimage to the place.

Moree is Kamilaroi country and the Moree Plains Gallery specialises in Aboriginal art, particularly expert woodcarvings. Just inside the main entrance is the striking Myall Tree, carved by well-known artist Lawrence White. If you like what you see, there are a couple of indigenous-art and clothing stores in and around Moree where you can pick up a gift or souvenir.

Glen Innes has another fine indigenous gallery, the Cooramah Aboriginal Cultural Centre, which also houses the Koori Cuisine restaurant. Try meals such as bush burgers with kangaroo and emu meat, vegetarian spinach-and-ricotta burgers and, if you're feeling brave, *witjutie* (witchetty) grub salad.

New England straddles the Great Dividing Range in New South Wales from northwest of Newcastle to the Queensland border.

WHEN
You can visit the region year-round, but country-music fans should plan a trip in late January to catch the Tamworth Country Music Festival, which invariably features a large contingent of indigenous musicians and singers.

HOW
Armidale's Aboriginal Cultural Centre & Keeping Place (02-6771 1249) displays art and artefacts from the New England region. You can also buy locally made Koori art-works, artefacts, didjeridus and jewellery.

In Gunnedah, at the edge of the Namoi Valley, Red Chief Local Aboriginal Land Council (02-6742 3602) runs full- or half-day tours to significant rock paintings, tree carvings and *bora* (ceremonial) grounds. Gunnedah is also popular with koalas – look out for them in and around town.

The Willows, a 1400-hectare property on the Severn River about thirty-five kilometres northwest of Glen Innes, has guided walks to tell you about the Aboriginal culture of the area, as well as bush-tucker and dance displays. Bookings can be made at Cooramah Aboriginal Cultural Centre (02-6732 5960).

Antarctic beech forest at Weeping, New England National Park
Photo: Richard I'Anson

Further north, near Tenterfield, is Australia's largest granite monolith. Bald Rock was a neutral meeting ground for three tribes: the Githabal in the northeast, the Dingghabal in the north and the Wahlebal in the south. The largely treeless, smooth appearance of Bald Rock has been likened to Uluru but, unlike Uluru, it is appropriate (and fun) to climb to the top.

Walcha town sign Photo: Ian Connellan

Each experience for me
brings out a deeper sense of
this country and its history,
how these people live on it
and maintain it, the pride.
— Cath

Blue Mountains haze melts into a pink sunset: the view from Echo Point **Photo:** Ross Barnett

Mountain Myths:
Blue Mountains

One of the most popular day trips for Sydney-siders, the Blue Mountains are a breath of crisp, fresh air, with fantastic bushwalking and rock-climing for adrenaline junkies, and Devonshire tea and Art Deco architecture thrown in for good measure. The blue haze, which gave the mountains their name, is a result of the ultra-fine oily mist given off by eucalyptus trees. This haze, seen from a distance, makes the ranges look serenely blue.

Part of the Great Dividing Range that wends its way down the east of Australia, the mountains were initially an impenetrable barrier to white expansion from Sydney. Despite many attempts to find a route through the range – and a bizarre belief among many convicts that China, and freedom, was just on the other side – it took twenty-five years before a successful crossing was made by Europeans. A road was built soon afterwards that opened the western plains to settlement.

The Dharug people, who lived here around 15,000 years ago, are the custodians of the region. The beautiful peaks are thickly woven with Aboriginal legends, and perhaps the most famous is the tale of the Three Sisters – the impressive pillars of rock that can be seen from Echo Point in Katoomba, the touristy heart of the Blue Mountains. The story goes that the three sisters were turned to stone by a sorcerer to protect them from the unwanted advances of three young men, but the sorcerer died before he could turn them back into humans. Floodlit at night, the rocks are an awesome sight.

The mountains offer many opportunities to learn about indigenous culture first-hand. Muru Mittigar is an Aboriginal arts and cultural centre in Cranebrook, at the foot of the mountains. Activities include sampling bush tucker, dance performances, a native-plants nursery and a handicraft shop.

Blue gum forest in the Grose Valley **Photo:** Chris Bell

The Three Sisters who were turned to stone **Photo:** Dallas Stribley

In Blue Mountains National Park, the excellent Red Hands Cave walk takes you from Glenbrook Causeway to a sandstone shelter with coloured images of human hands. Drawn about 1600 years ago, these orange, red and white ochre outlines and filled-in images are among the best examples of this type of art near Sydney. European settlers stumbled upon the cave in 1913 while looking for a lost child around Glenbrook Creek. En route you'll pass an axe-grinding site.

In Kanangra Boyd National Park, the Jenolan Caves are Australia's best-known limestone caves. One cave has been open to the public since 1867, though parts of the system are still unexplored.

The cascading Wentworth Falls **Photo:** Mark Newman

WHERE
The Blue Mountains are fifty kilometres west of Sydney.

WHEN
You can visit throughout the year, but remember it's always a little cooler here than on the coast. The wildflower season is from September to October. In autumn (March to May) mists and drizzle can make bushwalking less attractive.

HOW
Aboriginal Blue Mountains Walkabout (0408 443 822) offers inspiring and physically challenging adventures, taking in an ancient cultural rite of passage along a songline (Dreaming track) of the Oryang-Ora people.

Muru Mittigar (02-4729 2377), in Cranebrook, runs Aboriginal history tours.

At the Mount Tomah Botanic Gardens (02-4567 2154), in Mount Tomah, you can take an exclusive ecotour into a closed conservation area (only one group is allowed per day).

Aussie Bushabout Holidays (0408 695 958) specialises in bushwalking ecotourism, and works with indigenous guides from the Burramadine Aboriginal Corporation.

The Discovery programme (02-4787 8877) of the Department of Environment and Conservation (DEC) employs a number of Aboriginal rangers, and groups can arrange tours to Aboriginal sites on request.

Music & Dance

Song and dance pervade every aspect of daily life for indigenous Australians. These art forms traditionally close the gap between space and time, providing a door to the Dreaming (p16).

Songlines, also known as Dreaming tracks, follow the journey of the spirit ancestors during the Dreaming as they sang up the country into life and act as musical maps of a particular area's landscape. A singer can describe the country through the rhythm of a song, which changes to describe hills or lakes and rivers. The beat of the song will tell the knowledgeable listener what is in the land. Such songs are inherited and carry important social obligations from the song's owner. Other songs are performed within specific day-to-day contexts providing a vital connection with the spirit world, such as during childbirth or mourning, to direct a soul to its destination. Songs are also thought of as 'medicine', as they can be healing. They can be used to bring rain, stop floods, change the direction of the wind, or sing a heat wave. More recently, traditional music has merged with Western styles – such as folk, country and rock – for sheer entertainment.

Indigenous musical instruments are usually made from natural resources. Traditional instruments therefore vary from region to region according to available materials. Percussion instruments are variously made from selected woods, shells and stones, and specially shaped clapsticks or message sticks, which are hit together to make different pitches. The Yirkala Mirning community (a coastal tribe from the Nullarbor Plain) for example, creates a variety of tones by hitting together 'gong stones' of different shapes and sizes, gathered from the caves and cliff faces around the Great Australian Bight. This music communicates with the southern right and sperm whales, calling them into the bight.

The haunting resonance of the didjeridu is perhaps the most iconic sound of Aboriginal music. The didj originated in Arnhem Land, at the top end of the Northern Territory, and its Yolngu name is *yidaki*. Didjeridus are made from particular eucalypt branches that have been hollowed out by termites. They are cut down to a metre or more in length and then carved and shaped so they fit in the palm of your hand. They are then fitted with a wax mouthpiece made from sugarbag (native honeybee wax) and decorated with traditional designs.

The main instrument of the Torres Strait Islands is a skin-covered drum, which is held in one hand while the palm of

the other hand is used to create a deep rhythmic pounding sound that echoes hypnotically. The *kulup* is a hand shaker made of black seeds tied together with a special twine from the islands to imitate the sound of shells being shaken. The Islanders are also known for the beautiful harmonies of the men and women singing traditional or gospel-influenced songs.

Music and songs accompany dancing, which is integral to Aboriginal and Torres Strait Islander culture, a physical and spiritual expression of indigenous norms, religion and stories, and an essential part of ceremonies. A dance performance will tell a story of the Dreaming, an ancestor spirit or the passing down of a law. In keeping with animist traditions, many dancers imitate the movements and sounds of the spirit ancestor's animal form. Dancers often decorate their bodies with paint, with particular designs distinguishing social standing.

Dance styles vary across regions and tribes. Most dances are accompanied by singing, percussion instruments (such as clapsticks or boomerangs) or hand and thigh clapping. The didjeridu provides music to the fast-moving 'shake-a-leg' dance of Cape York Peninsula and the rhythmic stomp of Arnhem Land. In the Torres Strait, the energising militaristic style reveals strong Polynesian influences.

Dance is a communal event in which every member of the clan participates. Children learn dance and song at an early age and are expected to perform during certain ceremonies. Sacred initiation ceremonies for young boys and girls are great communal celebrations of singing, dancing and music. Other dances are gender based, such as fertility rituals for women, when members of the opposite sex do not see each other's performances. Dancing is also part of death rituals.

Contemporary indigenous dance combines traditional and Western dance styles and draws on tradtional and contemporary themes in movement, stories, costume and body art, fusing music and song. This unique and mesmerising blend of dance can be seen in performances by various troupes, including the Bangarra Dance Theatre, the country's premier indigenous dance company. Credited with international and Olympic performances, Bangarra has collaborated with the Australian Ballet in *Rites*, an acclaimed work blending two different cultural expressions in movement.

Old-time shops in the rural town of Gulgong Photo: Claver Carroll

The Story of Scar Trees:
Central West NSW & Riverina

The plains of central west New South Wales are steeped in gold-rush and bushranger history, while the Riverina is a fertile land of green, rolling countryside fed by the mighty Murrumbidgee River.

This is Wiradjuri country and most visitors come here to prowl through Dubbo's Western Plains Zoo (Australia's largest open-range zoo) or learn about star-gazing via the huge radio telescope at Parkes. But there's also a great opportunity to learn about Wiradjuri scar trees and their role in traditional life.

At museums in Orange and Dubbo you can see carved trees on display, but it's well worth making the effort to track down a scar tree in the countryside. Scar trees were carefully selected and their bark was removed using a stone axe, leaving the scar. The bark was then treated, usually with

fire, to make canoes, dishes, shields and other items. The trees are often identifiable by a telltale notch just below the main scar, which was used as a foothold.

Northwest of Orange, off the Mitchell Highway, is the grave of Yuranigh, a Wiradjuri man who acted as a guide on many expeditions of explorer and surveyor Major Thomas Mitchell. Mitchell held Yuranigh's skill, courage and honesty in very high regard, and described him in his journal as his 'guide, companion, counsellor and friend'. As well as a European headstone, the site is marked by four decorative memorial scar trees, which demonstrate his similar repute among the local Aborigines.

Another interesting grave is that of Ben Hall, a landowner who became Australia's first official bushranger, and who was betrayed and shot near the town of Forbes. He's buried

WHERE
The central west of New South Wales stretches 400 kilometres inland from the Blue Mountains, changing from fields to plains and finally to the harsh outback. The Riverina, to the south, encompasses the area fed by the Murrumbidgee River.

WHEN
Autumn (March to May) and spring (September to November) are the most comfortable times to visit the region.

HOW
At Narrandera in the Riverina, Sandhills Artefacts (02-6959 2593) can tailor a tour to meet your interests and available time. You can experience an interpretive guide to local sites and feast on fresh bush tucker. Tours range from two hours to one week. A trip along the Murrumbidgee River can also be organised. Prices (on application) depend on numbers and the extent of the tour.

Riverina wheat crop ready for harvest **Photo:** Claver Carroll

in the town's cemetery; people still miss him, if the notes on his grave are anything to go by. Hall had been falsely accused of being involved in a hold-up, and while he was in jail his wife ran off with another man, his house was burned down and his cattle disappeared, and these miserable circumstances forced him into a life of crime.

Ancient rock paintings depicting hand stencils by Aboriginal visitors over the millennia can be seen at the Drip (also known as Hands on Rock), about forty kilometres northwest of Gulgong. You can camp at this water hole, which is west of Goulburn River National Park.

Quaint houses in Gulgong **Photo:** Claver Carroll

Platypus nosing amongst the grass **Photo:** Simon Foale

Indoor & Outdoor Galleries: Australian Capital Territory

Canberra's museums and galleries are a superb, refined introduction to indigenous art and culture, but the Australian Capital Territory offers fine art in the fresh air, too.

Canberra's highlights include the Australian National Gallery, where you can see major works by many of Australia's most prominent indigenous artists; the National Museum of Australia; and the Australian Institute of Aboriginal and Torres Strait Islander Studies Library.

But for a real taste of traditional life, strap on your walking boots and visit Namadgi National Park. The Yankee Hat Walk in this park south of Canberra takes you to a gallery of paintings by the Ngunnawal people.

The ranges here have been profoundly important to the Ngunnawal people for thousands of years. There is evidence

at nearby Birrigai of Aboriginal occupation dating back 21,000 years (the last ice age), and the area is a rich source of food, including snakes, platypuses, water birds and Bogong moths. It's likely that Aboriginal people stayed in this area to feast on the moths, which migrate here in late spring, and may have used the shelter as a base and meeting ground.

The Yankee Hat paintings, the largest collection in Namadgi, are grouped together low down on a big rounded granite boulder, one of several in a cluster overlooked by Yankee Hat mountain (the name of a nearby peak that looks like an American colonial hat). Faint red-brown figures are the oldest, while the lighter-coloured ones are the most recent. Ochre was used to make red paint, clay for white; they were turned into a paste by adding water, sap, animal oils or blood. Most of the figures are either abstract images or rep-

Giant boulders and delicate wildflowers, Kosciusko National Park. **Photo:** Rob Blakers

Early morning mist hovers over Lake Burley Griffin, Canberra. **Photo:** Karen Trist

WHERE
Namadgi National Park is the northernmost park in the Australian Alps and is just thirty kilometres south of Canberra, in the Australian Capital Territory.

WHEN
Snow can fall over any part of the park in winter, which is nice if you're a cross-country skier, but for bushwalking it's better to visit in summer (December to February). Bring warm and waterproof clothing at any time of year.

HOW
The Yankee Hat Walk brochure is available from the Environment ACT website (www.environment.act.gov.au/bushparksand reserves/namadgi.html). Information on guided activities in Namadgi National Park is available from the visitors centre, two kilometres south of Tharwa.

For more information about the Australian National Gallery check out their website at www.nga.gov.au; for the National Museum of Australia go to www.nma.gov.au; and for the Australian Institute of Aboriginal and Torres Strait Islander Studies Library visit www.aiatsis.gov.au.

resentations of humans; others resemble dingoes and possibly kangaroos, wombats or koalas, echidnas or turtles, and emus or brolgas. The walk is an easy six-kilometre trek that starts and finishes at the car park by Old Boboyan Road.

If you've still got itchy feet after you've done the walk, head over to the Australian National Botanic Gardens for the Aboriginal Plant Use Walk, or to Yass for the Ngunnawal Walk around Riverbank Park on the Yass River.

Indigenous plants at the Australian National Botanic Gardens, Canberra. **Photo:** Richard Nebesky

Sunlit river gums reflecting in the Murray at Bruce's Bend **Photo:** John Hay

The Kakadu of the South: Murray River

The mighty Murray River weaves a lazy course covering 2700 kilometres, taking in snowy mountains, wetlands and fertile agricultural country. Each environment has its own story to tell, just as it did thousands of years ago, when the river's rich food resources made this area one of the most densely populated parts of Australia.

A tour along the Murray River will take you past some superb cultural centres to learn about Aboriginal life on the river. A good way to start is by joining the Murray Outback Aboriginal Cultural Trail (which includes parts of Victoria, New South Wales and South Australia) in Swan Hill. It's a self-drive trail that will take you to keeping places (cultural centres), tour operators, art galleries and sacred sites.

Follow the river east for a real cultural treat in Yorta Yorta country. Known as the Kakadu of the south, but without the

crocodiles, Barmah State Park is a significant wetland area created by the flood plains of the Murray River between Echuca and Tocumwal. It's the largest remaining red-gum forest in Australia (and thus the world), and the swampy understorey is usually flooded in winter, creating a complex wetland ecology that is an important breeding area for many fish and bird species. The forest holds special significance for the Yorta Yorta, whose ancestors have lived in the area for 40,000 years. Within the forest are middens, oven mounds and scar trees.

For a wonderful introduction to local Aboriginal culture, visit the Dharnya Centre (run by members of the Yorta Yorta people in partnership with Parks Victoria) in Barmah State Park, or head southeast to Shepparton's Bangerang Keeping Place. Both centres have Yorta Yorta cultural officers who can suggest trails through the magnificent Barmah forest.

Rollin' on the river: the Murray River Marathon
Photo: Phil Weymouth

Walkers can pick up the interesting Wirad-juri Walkabout walking track along the river between Albury and Wodonga, or head twelve kilomtres north of Beechworth to Mount Pilot. Here you'll find the terrific Yeddonba Aboriginal Rock Art Walking Trail (on Toveys Road, off the Chiltern–Beechworth Road). This forty-five-minute, self-guided round route gives an insight into the local Duduroa clan. The rock art at Yeddonba features faded paintings of a Tasmanian tiger, a lizard and a snake.

Tree skeleton beside Lake Crosbie Photo: Paul Sinclair

WHERE
The Murray River starts in the Snowy Mountains and for most of its length forms the boundary between New South Wales and Victoria. It then meanders for 650 kilometres through South Australia (see p216).

WHEN
Albury is famous for the Mungabareena Ngan Girra Festival, which has a 20,000-year (plus!) history and takes place during the last week of November at the Mungabareena Reserve. Each year, the indigenous people of the area would meet at Mungabareena before journeying north into the high country to feast upon the delectable Bogong moth.

HOW
The Dharnya Centre (03-5869 3302), in Barmah State Park, has information about the forest and the Murray River as well as about the history and culture of the indige-nous people of the area. They can also advise on activities within the park, including bushwalking, bird-watching, wetland cruises, canoeing, fishing and cycling.

The Bangerang Keeping Place (03-5831 1020) in Shepparton has a good collection of Koorie art and artefacts, which help explain the rich culture of the local people.

For a tour of significant Aboriginal sites in Barmah State Park, and a spot of bird-watching, try a two-hour wetland cruise aboard the cruise boat *Kingfisher* (03-5869 3399).

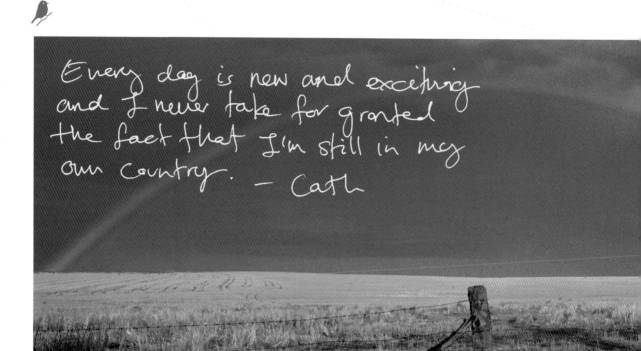

Every day is new and exciting and I never take for granted the fact that I'm still in my own country. — Cath

A rainbow arcs over Wimmera wheat fields **Photo:** Patrick Horton

Bunjil's Sacred Home: The Wimmera

Mount Arapiles is the Wimmera's most celebrated attraction – it's world-famous as Australia's best rock-climbing site. The agricultural plains of the Wimmera feature in mission history and are home to important rock-art and archaeological sites. This area was also the training ground for Australia's first international cricket team – an all-Aboriginal squad that toured England in 1868.

South of the town of Stawell is Bunjil's Shelter, one of the most significant Aboriginal rock-art sites in southern Australia. Bunjil is the Koorie Creator spirit, and the painting, enclosed in a protective wire grill, is enhanced by the contours of the rock. Although there are interpretive signs, it's much more interesting to visit the site on a cultural tour.

To the southeast, Langi Ghiran State Park also has some important art sites. Langi Ghiran is derived from an Abori-

ginal name for the home of the black cockatoo, which is found here along with many other species of birds, including corellas, robins, honeyeaters and finches. The Lar-ne-Jeering Walking Track, in the southeast of the park, takes you to an Aboriginal shelter with rock art unique to the area.

North of the Grampians, Ebenezer Mission, near Dimboola, was established by Moravian missionaries in 1859 and operated until 1904. As with other missions, the central – misguided – aim at Ebenezer was to 'civilise' the indigenous population by means of school and church services and by banning traditional practices such as corroborees. These historic buildings are the oldest surviving mission buildings in Victoria. Although once in ruins, they have now been classified by the National Trust and are undergoing restoration.

World-class rock climbing at Mount Arapiles Photo: Jonathan Chester

A Southern Cross windmill backlit by a rainbow Photo: Patrick Horton

Mount Arapiles-Tooan Park (known as Djurite to indigenous people), a state park about thirty kilometres west of
Horsham, is a hot destination for rock-climbers. They come
here from all around the world and on most days you can
see them – or join them – scaling the mountain.

The park also has around forty-two identified Aboriginal
archaeological sites as well as scar trees and rock art,
though not all sites are open to the public. The traditional
owners of this land are the Djurid balug clan and this area
is still of great significance to Aboriginal people.

Further south at Harrow, near Edenhope, the Johnny Mullagh Cricket Centre tells the story of the 1868 Aboriginal
cricket team. Harrow is Mullagh's home town and the town
enthusiastically celebrates its famous son.

WHERE
The Wimmera is in western
Victoria, about 250 kilo-
metres west of Melbourne.

WHEN
Cricket fans should come
on the Labour Day weekend
(the second Monday in
March) to see an Aboriginal
XI take on a Glenelg XI for
the Johnny Mullagh Shield
at Harrow. Spring is the
best time for bird-watching
at Langi Ghiran.

HOW
The area is easily explored
in your own vehicle, but
you'll get a better insight
into local sites with an
Aboriginal guide. The
Brambuk Aboriginal
Cultural Centre (03-5356
4452) in Halls Gap (p214)
conducts a range of tours
to local indigenous sites,
including Bunjil's Shelter.
Bookings must be made
at least a day in advance
and some tours require a
minimum of three people.
Aboriginal Dreamtime Trails
(03-5342 8788) also runs
tours to local sites.

White-clay paintings at the Ngamadjidj Shelter in the Grampians National Park **Photo:** Richard I'Anson

Wonderland of Wildflowers & Rock Art: Grampians National Park

The Grampians are one of Victoria's most outstanding natural features and a wonderland of flora and fauna. The array of attractions includes an incredibly rich diversity of wildlife and plant species, spectacular wildflower displays, unique and unusual rock formations and a trickling network of creeks, streams, cascades and waterfalls.

Understandably, this beautiful place is of huge significance to local Aboriginal communities and there are many important rock-art sites (the largest collection in southern Australia) and sacred places within the park. The Aboriginal name for the area is Gariwerd.

Your first port of call should be the attractive Brambuk Aboriginal Cultural Centre in Halls Gap. It's run collectively by five Koorie communities. Many features of the interior design are symbolic: the curved seat just inside the entrance represents the caring embrace of the Creator spirit Bunjil, the ramp upstairs is the eel Dreaming, while the theatre ceiling depicts the southern right whale (totem of the Gunditjmara people). Inside there's an exhibition area, shop, café and performance space; a wide range of activities are also on offer.

But don't leave the park before visiting at least one of the rock-art sites. There is an extensive collection within the Grampians National Park, but not all of it is publicised or accessible. In the Northern Grampians near Mount Stapylton the main sites are Gulgurn Manja Shelter and Ngamadjidj Shelter. In the Western Grampians, near the Buandik camping ground, the main sites are Billimina Shelter and Manja Shelter. These rock paintings were made with either ochre or white clay, and are mostly drawings or stencils such as hand prints, animal tracks or stick figures.

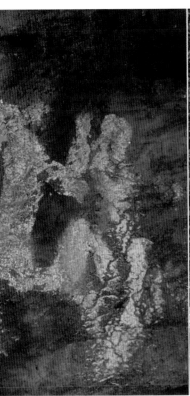

Pink sundew flowers sprouting through a carpet of moss Photo: Sally Dillon

Red gums emerging from the morning mist
Photo: Paul Sinclair

The walks to the sites are part of the attraction. Over 900 species of native trees,
shrubs and wildflowers have been recorded
here and there are almost 200 species of
birds, thirty-five different mammals and
twenty-eight reptiles, so you never know
what you might see in your wanderings.

The park is also a centre for adventure
sports, including rock climbing, abseiling,
canoeing and caving.

The craggy Balconies overhang in the Grampians National Park
Photo: Paul Sinclair

WHERE
The Grampians National
Park is in the Wimmera
(p212), 260 kilometres
(three-and-a-half hours'
drive) west of Melbourne,
Victoria.

WHEN
The mountains are at their
best in spring, when the
wildflowers (including
twenty species that don't
exist anywhere else in the
world) are at their peak.
However, the Grampians
are worth visiting at any
time of year, although it
can often be extremely hot
in summer and very wet in
winter.

HOW
The best place to go for
information is the Brambuk
Aboriginal Cultural Centre
(03-5356 4452). The
centre offers a wide range
of performances and tours
to local indigenous sites
with an Aboriginal guide,
and this is far more rewarding than visiting them
independently.

Just near Brambuk is
the helpful Grampians
National Park Visitor Centre
(03-5356 4381). It has
indigenous displays and
sells good maps indicating
walking trails to Aboriginal
rock-art sites.

A russet Murray River bank tinged by sunset in Murray-Kulkyne State Park **Photo:** Richard I'Anson

Hidden Treasure-Troves of Rock Art: Lower Murray River

There are few things as relaxing as floating down the Murray River on a boat cruise. And if you're interested in rock art, this area has some well-kept secrets.

For over 40,000 years the Lower Murray River has been a major source of fresh water, fish, plants and bark (for canoes) for the Meru people. They settled along its banks in comparatively large numbers. Some of the cliffs between Mannum, east of Adelaide, and Berri, near the Victorian border, are rich in rock art (most of which is off-limits), and hundreds of scarred gum trees dot the riverbanks, especially along the eastern side of the Murray, opposite Blanchetown.

Ngaut Ngaut Conservation Park is one of Australia's most significant archaeological sites and one of the few places you can see examples of this rock art. Visits to the site are

carefully controlled. As the centre of Wumbulgal Purka Bidni (Black Duck Dreaming), the park is sacred to the Meru and Ngarrindjeri people. In 1929, a 7000-year-old skeleton of a young boy was discovered here, and remains of campfires and burial sites, as well as stunning rock art, clearly indicate several temporary settlements. Of major interest are carvings of dolphins, which may have once swum this far inland.

The park is just off the road along the eastern bank of the Murray, between Purnong and Nildottie. It is not signposted, and individual entry is not permitted – all visitors must be part of a guided tour.

Southwest of Purnong is picturesque Mannum, where the *Mary Ann*, Australia's first riverboat, was built in 1853 and made the first paddle-steamer trip up the Murray. At

216

A paddle steamer moored at the river bank Photo: Dallas Stribley

the Mannum visitors centre you'll find the Mannum Dock Museum of River History, which features the restored 1897 paddle steamer PS *Marion*. There are also displays about the Ngarrindjeri Aboriginal communities and the Dreaming story of Pondi, the giant Murray cod. According to legend, Ngurundjeri, the Dreaming ancestor of the Ngarrindjeri, was fishing one day when he saw Pondi and chased it down the Murray River, then only a small creek. As the fish swam away, its tail thrashed from side to side, widening the river and creating cliffs and lagoons.

Historic Railway Terrace in the town of Morgan
Photo: Denis O'Byrne

WHERE
The Lower Murray River flows through South Australia's Riverland, heading west from the Victorian border to Morgan before turning south towards Lake Alexandrina.

WHEN
The Riverland can get fiendishly hot in summer (December to February). Many people like to visit from August to November to see magnificent wildflowers in bloom.

HOW
Ngaut Ngaut can only be visited with a guide. Tours are operated by Aboriginal Elder Richard Hunter (08-8570 1202), and are included in the expensive but delightful two- to five-day boat cruises on PS *Murray Princess* (08-8569 2511). Cheaper tours may be available if you contact Hunter and time a visit to the park to coincide with a tour by boat passengers.

The Pomberuk Indigenous Cultural Centre in Murray Bridge is housed in the historic Old Pumphouse building on the banks of the Murray River. The centre offers tours and has a gallery featuring work by local Ngarrindjeri artists; you can also sample traditional foods at the Pomberuk Bush Tucker Bistro.

River-cruise and houseboat bookings can be made at the Mannum visitors centre (08-8569 1303).

217

Ghostly gums lining a dry creek bed frame a Flinders Ranges peak Photo: Richard I'Anson

Ochre Dreaming: Flinders Ranges

The stunning red and purple folds of the Flinders Ranges combine with the deep blue sky, golden grasses and sage-green vegetation to create one of the most beautiful places in Australia. The colours shift with changes in the light and this is no place to forget your camera!

Rich in indigenous heritage, this area is particularly easy to access, with plenty of cultural tours, information about Flinders Ranges National Park and lots of resource books available at visitors centres. So slap on some sunscreen and get ready to learn about giant snakes, bearded dragons and the all-important ochre trade.

Flinders Ranges National Park, in the southern end of the ranges, is home to the iconic Wilpena Pound. This natural basin is sacred to the Adnyamathanha (Hills People), who have lived in the area for over 15,000 years. The

Adnyamathanha name for Wilpena Pound is Ikara, and Dreaming stories tell of two *akurra* (giant snakes), who coiled around Ikara during an initiation ceremony, creating a whirlwind and devouring most of the participants. The snakes were so full after their feast they could not move and willed themselves to die, thus creating the landmark. Because of its traditional significance, the Adnyamathanha prefer that visitors don't climb Saint Mary Peak (Ngarri Mudlanha), which is reputed to be the head of the female snake.

Arkaroo Rock was first occupied over 6000 years ago, and initiation ceremonies were still being held here in the 1940s. The rock shelter boasts numerous paintings of reptiles, leaves and human figures created with yellow and red ochre, charcoal and bird lime, which explain, among other things, the formation of Wilpena Pound.

Glowing tree in Wilpena Pound **Photo:** Paul Sinclair

Sacred Canyon is home to more than one hundred Adnyamathanha rock engravings featuring abstract designs and animal tracks, many with unusually large circles.

To the south of the park you can visit the seven-metre-high quartzite boulder called Death Rock. It overlooks the pretty Kanyaka Waterhole, and, according to one story, local Adnyamathanha people would place their dying kinsfolk here to see out their last hours.

A little north of here are the marvellous Yourambulla Caves. The Adnyamathanha name for the caves, Yuralypila, means 'Two Men', and refers to the twin peaks to the east. Although probably never inhabited, the

Adnyamathanha rock art **Photo:** Christopher Groenhout

WHERE
The Flinders Ranges rise from the northern end of the Spencer Gulf in South Australia and run 400 kilometres north into the arid outback.

WHEN
Autumn (March to May) is a comfortable time to visit, with mild days and cool nights, while winter (June to August) is better for wildlife-watching. Avoid the hot summer months (December to February).

HOW
Iga Warta (08-8648 3737) is an impressive outfit owned and operated by Adnyamathanha people. It offers a number of cultural tours and walks to local sites, overnight tours to Red Gorge and campfire evenings with Dreaming stories, indigenous music and bush tucker. Also available are courses in Aboriginal art and horse riding.

The Aboriginal-owned and -operated Fray Cultural Tours (08-8648 4303), based in Hawker, offers a range of tours throughout the Flinders region.

Arkaba Trail Rides, run by an Adnyamathanha Elder, offers tours on horseback to important burial and art sites (among other places) in and around Arkaba Station. Contact the Wilpena Pound Visitor Centre (08-8648 0048) for bookings.

The National Parks and Wildlife South Australia (NWPSA) organises various tours and walks during

(continued on p221)

The ancient weathered cliffs of Wilpena Pound **Photo:** Paul Sinclair

White stripes: Adnyamathanha rock painting **Photo:** John Hay

caves boast a collection of detailed rock art, such as emu tracks, that explain several Dreaming stories. Surprisingly, most of the art here is painted with black dyes rather than the red ochre that is so important in this region.

Ochre is more than just a pigment to the Adnyamathanha. There are many valuable sources of high-quality red ochre in the Flinders Ranges, used for artistic, ceremonial and medicinal purposes. The ochre and pituri, a mildly narcotic drug, were traded across the continent, as were stones for axes and tools, and shells for decoration.

The trade in ochre made the Adnyamathanha people comparatively prosperous, and the ochre itself is of great spiritual importance. Traditional stories explain that the vivid orange colour of the landscape is from Marrukurli, dangerous dogs who were killed by Adnu, the bearded dragon. When Adnu killed the black Marrukurli, the sun went out and he was forced to throw his boomerang in every direction to reawaken the sun. It was only when he threw it to the east that the sun returned. Meanwhile the blood of the Marrukurli had seeped into the earth to create sacred ochre deposits.

You can learn more about Adnyamathanha culture at Iga Warta, in the northern Flinders Ranges. South of here is Mount Chambers – known to the Adnyamathanha as Wadna Yaldha Vambata (Boomerang Crack Hill). It features galleries of rock carvings, often produced by pecking at the surface with a hard rock. Interestingly, many of the carvings feature the sorts of circles and lines found near Uluru (Ayers Rock; p88), and relate Creation legends – that of Wilpena Pound, for example. Particularly impressive are the engravings in a small gorge before the main Chambers Gorge.

the Easter and September school holidays using Adnyamathanha guides, which focus on places such as Sacred Canyon. Aboriginal art lessons and campfires with Dreaming stories are also available. Contact the Wilpena Pound Visitor Centre for details and bookings.

Leigh Creek Station (about six kilometres east of Leigh Creek) runs various cultural tours with Adnyamathanha guides, including to Red Gorge, which is on private property. It also offers horse riding and budget-priced accommodation. Contact the Leigh Creek Visitors Centre (08-8675 2723) for more details and bookings.

There are excellent information boards set up around the ranges to tell you about local Aboriginal culture. You can also pick up one of the Dreaming trails, which are explained in the helpful brochure *South Australian Aboriginal Dreaming of the Flinders Ranges*, available at the region's visitors centres. The trails themselves take in Iga Warta, Arkaroola (a wildlife sanctuary near the northern end of the Flinders Ranges) and other sacred sites in the Flinders.

A rocky outcrop meets wind-streaked clouds **Photo:** Greg Elms

Grass trees stand sentinel amongst rocks **Photo:** Paul Sinclair

Index

Going Bush: Adventures Across Indigenous Australia
January 2006

Published by
Lonely Planet Publications Pty Ltd ABN 36 005 607 983
90 Maribyrnong St, Footscray, Victoria 3011, Australia

www.lonelyplanet.com
AOL keyword: lp

Printed through Colorcraft Ltd, Hong Kong
Printed in China

ISBN 1 74104 736 6

Authors
The text was written by lead author Monique Choy, with contributing authors Brigitte Barta, David Collins, Meg Worby, Charles Rawlings-Way, Simone Egger, Rachael Antony, David Andrew, Jane Ormond and Alex Landragin. The text in this book is based on Lonely Planet's guidebooks, which are researched and written by a global team of authors.

Credits
This book was commissioned in Lonely Planet's Melbourne office by Bridget Blair, under the direction of Publishing Manager Chris Rennie and Publisher Roz Hopkins. It was based on the Lonely Planet Television series *Going Bush*.

Production Manager: Jo Vraca
Project Manager: Jenny Bilos
Designers: Steven Caddy and Daniel New
Layout Designer: Vicki Beale
Editors: Adrienne Costanzo assisted by Martine Lleonart
Image Research: Ellen Burrows
Pre-press Production: Ryan Evans
Cartographers: Paul Piaia assisted by Emma McNicol
Print Production: Graham Imeson

Thanks to Laurence Billiet, David Collins and Joany Sze of Lonely Planet Television; Francesca Coles, Wibowo Rusli, John Shippick and Pablo Garcia Gastar

Photographs
Many of the images in this book are available for licensing from Lonely Planet Images: www.lonelyplanetimages.com

Front cover photographs (digital composition): Michael Hutchinson/Short St Gallery, Peter Solness, Patrick Horton, Daniel New
Back cover photograph: Rob Blakers
pp 8-9; 16-17; 18-19; 74; 92-3; 152; 180-1: Peter Solness
pp 10-11: Regis Martin
pp 46-7; 204-5: Oliver Strewe
pp 64-5: Peter Ptschelinzew
pp 114-15: Lawrie Williams
pp 166-7; 182-3: Richard I'Anson

The *Going Bush* TV series was developed with the support of Aboriginal Tourism Australia.

Principal investors: FFC and Film Victoria

Lonely Planet Offices

Australia
90 Maribyrnong St, Footscray, Victoria, 3011
tel: 03 8379 8000
fax: 03 8379 8111
email: talk2us@lonelyplanet.com.au

USA
150 Linden St, Oakland, CA 94607
tel: 510 893 8555 TOLL FREE: 800 275 8555
fax: 510 893 8572
email: info@lonelyplanet.com

UK
72-82 Rosebery Ave, London EC1R 4RW
tel: 020 7841 9000
fax: 020 7841 9001
email: go@lonelyplanet.co.uk